VANITY CIRCUS

A Smart Girl's Guide to Avoid Publishing Crap

By
Michelle Gamble-Risley and Michele Smith

3L Publishing
Sacramento, California
©2010. All Rights Reserved

Vanity Circus
A Smart Girl's Guide to Avoid Publishing Crap

Copyright © 2010 by Michelle Gamble-Risley and Michele Smith. All rights reserved. No part of this book may be reproduced or transmitted in any form or by any means, electronic or mechanical, including photocopying, recording, or by any information storage and retrieval system, without the written permission of the publisher except in the case of brief quotations, or except where permitted by law.

The information contained in this book is intended to be educational and not for diagnosis, prescription, or treatment of any business disorder whatsoever. This book is sold with the understanding that neither the author nor publisher is engaged in rendering any legal, psychological, or accounting advice. The publisher and author disclaim personal liability, directly or indirectly, for advice of information presented within. Although the author and publisher have prepared this manuscript with utmost care and diligence and have made every effort to ensure the accuracy and completeness of the information contained within, we assume no responsibility for errors, inaccuracies, omissions, or inconsistencies.

Library of Congress Control Number: 2010926997

ISBN-13: 978-0-615-37012-5

3L Publishing soft-cover edition April 2010.

Printed in the United States of America.

Book design by Erin Pace.

*To my two beautiful children, Cole and Cambria.
I know you sacrifice "mommy" time so I can be more than
just your mommy. I love you both with all my heart!
~ Michelle Gamble-Risley*

*To my little boy Dylan ... you make me laugh just as hard
as all of the bad manuscripts.
~ Michele Smith*

Table of Contents

Acknowledgments iii

Introduction v

Chapter 1: The Good, The Bad and The Brutally Ugly 1

Chapter 2: Why We Rejected "Shattered Lives" Part 10 …
Or Rejection Hurts Both of Us 5

Chapter 3: Book Covers that Rock or Suck! 13

Chapter 4: The Book as Platform — A Winning Outlook on Publishing 17

Chapter 5: Self-Publishing, Vanity Press or Do-It-Yourself-ers 23

Chapter 6: Traditional Publishing: "Oh Toto! We're Not in
Kansas Anymore." 31

Chapter 7: Hybrid Publishers: Breaking all the Rules and Loving It 39

Chapter 8: Publish on Demand … You Didn't! Yes, You Did 47

Chapter 9: Agents: Get out of their Pockets … It Stinks Back Here 57

Chapter 10: Queries, Synopsis … the Necessary Evils 63

Chapter 11: Really?! If You Happen to get a Call-Back New Rules to Not act like an A$$ 69

Chapter 12: Finally! My Baby! Now What? Marketing Time! 77

Chapter 13: The Road to a Best-Selling Author is paved with Great Publicity 87

Chapter 14: Hey! That's My Copyright! Isn't it …?" 95

Love Letter 101

About the Authors 103

Acknowledgments

2L wishes to thank the following:

I would like to thank our always-faithful and hard-working graphic artist, Erin Pace, you are so talented and you make us look fantastic. I also wish to thank our photographer Gail Shoop-Lamy, you are funny and priceless. And a big thank you to my husband Russell Risley. I know you understand what it takes to be successful in this economy, and you've given me a lot of latitude to pursue my dreams. And finally to all of our amazing authors. You are all incredible talents who entrust your "babies" to us every day. We thank you so much for being a part of 3L Publishing. And last but not least, Malia Grigsby, our project manager who does the truly hard work that makes our operations run!

1L wishes to thank the following:

I would like to thank all of our wonderful authors who have embarked on this journey with us. Big hugs and kisses to my little Dylan, and thank you for always making me laugh — you are my whole world. I also would like to thank our graphic designer Erin Pace — your talent never ceases to amaze me and I always look forward to our projects together. Thank you to Malia Grigsby, our amazing project and operations manager — what would we ever do without you? Last, I would like to thank our photographer Gail Shoop-Lamy and our makeup artist Shannon Paige Nelson — you always make us look beautiful.

Introduction

You may wonder, "Why do I need this particular book on publishing when I can purchase one of hundreds of other books on the subject?" You're right the competition in the marketplace on the subject of publishing is pretty tight. You have "idiots" and "dummies" apparently all competing for your attention; but let's just say for a moment you're not an idiot or a dummy but a fairly smart and savvy writer and business person who would rather be called "smart" than stupid … and maybe you would even like to laugh a little while you learn. Does that sound like a much more interesting proposition? We think so.

We're smart girls, and we don't need to classify ourselves as idiots or dummies to learn a little something about our field of interest — and we would certainly rather be entertained than read yet another dry or boring book on publishing. Thus, you have a *Smart Girl's Guide to Avoid Publishing Crap* — and if that subtitle doesn't just shock you, make you laugh or at least giggle as you secretly think, "yep, understood," then we can't help you; but if you're ready to embrace the idea that you do not intend to publish anything that rhymes with "rap," we're all good. And if you're wondering why we would use such a profane word to describe a book — or if your upper-crust side thinks, "Oh my, did they really just say the word 'crap' on their book cover?!" And then you secretly stash away the book anyway — you friend are the exact demographic we want to read *Vanity Circus.*

And here is the real deal: Anyone familiar with publishing knows why we chose the title *Vanity Circus* too — because the industry has turned into an interesting and chaotic world filled with what we'll call lots of "clowns" and circus animals running amok from lack of true leadership, ingenuity or innovative thought. Old school traditional publishing is fraught with bureaucratic layers that add any number of expenses onto the process. Meanwhile, the days of lucrative advances have gone the way of the dinosaur petrified in La Brea tar pits, so no one really makes much money — and remember an advance goes against what royalties you can glean from the measly 10-15 percent you get *after* you buy your own books back off the shelf. Now combine this problem with the emergence of publish on demand and vanity presses that masquerade as publishing houses and rhyme with words like "zoolu" and "e-uni-curse" that have produced a spat of what we fondly call "crap."

And now you have an industry over populated with bad books and good books by authors who can't make a decent living unless they're a super star like Sarah Palin. Doesn't this all sound *special?* Now combine this problem with credibility lost because anyone with a buck in his or her pocket can publish anything on subjects as delightful as how to teach your frog to jump on command to Buck Jones eats squid while trying to row ashore. While vanity press spits out these amazing literary achievements, authors who invested perhaps thousands sit and eagerly await checks that amount to no more than $12 every six months ... but then again what do you expect when you name your book *Buck Jones and 12-Foot Squid Adventure* (that $12 probably came from your Mom who told her cousin to buy her daughter's book)? And why would you make decent royalties anyway when your book looks exactly like crap, reads like crap ... and in the end *smells* like crap? When no gatekeeper exists to vet the process and put standards or quality control in place — and allows any Joe or Sue to publish anything he or she wants to publish for a fee, of course, then what do you expect? Crap is crap by anybody's standards — and most consumers I know don't want to waste their hard-earned dollars on it.

So here we are spectators at the circus. We're eager to become a certified "ringleader" and don't know how. So, we're giving you *Vanity Circus* to guide you through what has essentially become a three-ring circus — traditional publishing on one end, publish on demand in the middle, and self publishing on the other end; but we have really terrific news for you. The true circus has come to town — and does have a ringleader. It provides a whole new way of publishing that — in our belief — will transform the industry and bring order to chaos. The new publishing that we are about to famously coin as the "Hybrid Model" offers solutions to resuscitate a dying industry. This new model developed by 3L Publishing, our company (we don't sound gratuitous now do we?) is changing the industry for the better.

As we begin to explore what we'll also call "New Publishing," we will take you through an in-depth overview of the publishing industry — and hopefully help you make educated and informed decisions. Since we're both writers, it kills us when authors arrive on our doorsteps with stories of thousands of dollars wasted because of ill-informed choices and common mistakes made out of pure lack of knowledge. At the same time, we don't want to bore you with the same old, same old lecture material you might be subjected to at a university class run by an instructor who has never published a book in his life ... but will give you a lot of smoke-and-mirrors information sure to send you screaming. I remember one professor who used to talk in circles about fiction. Literally talked in circles ... drove me absolutely nuts. I wanted to stand up — and if not for need of the credits would have — and shout, "Shut up! Shut up! Shut up!" Now I have to admit, a few authors drive me to distraction too. Oh, and I especially love it when they give me the blowhard story of why their crappy (we're going to use that word a lot in this book) manuscript is *soooo* good. And then argue with me for 10 minutes over their drivel-filled dialog. Gosh, it's so much fun to be a publisher! "I'm off to the see the wizard ..." And don't get me started on bad dialog. Ick! I've seen it all. "Gosh Jane did you see Spot run?"

So, *Vanity Circus* is going to teach smart girls — and boys if you can stand our chick-lit — how to not only write a book that sells, but also how to jump through hoops, maybe walk a tightrope or two, and tame the lion all while getting your book out there and sold. You will have a blast laughing as we describe why manuscripts end up in the ever-increasing rejection pile, and ultimately explain why the title "Shattered Lives" almost ended up as our title, *Don't Write 'Shattered Lives' If You want to be Published.* Oh, you would not believe how many books were bestowed that awful title in 2009. Seriously!! Not kidding.

So sit back, buckle up, and prepare to not "shatter" your manuscript. And hopefully when we're done you will understand what it takes to write a book that sells ... to more than your parents, family and friends.

Michelle (2L) Gamble-Risley

Just when I thought that we would not be doing another "side" project for awhile, 2L comes up with the great idea to publish *Vanity Circus: A Smart Girl's Guide to Avoid Publishing Crap,* and I could not have thought of a more relevant, fun project to be working on, because at 3L Publishing we do see a lot of crap. First, I must address the crap factor. We really do know that you should not be putting "crap" on the cover of your book, but my guess is if you are reading this you thought it was pretty funny — and so did we. Besides, if the media has a hissy fit over it we can always change it to "garbage."

The crap we receive at 3L comes in many forms. There are the multiple transcripts called *Shattered Lives* for one … umm, hello people? Someone may have trademarked that *popular* title — and you need to pick up the clue phone because it is ringing off the hook. Sadly, besides the title issue the content problem was also bad, bad and very bad.

Another form of crap is the complete lack of marketability of certain books. I think I have personally seen and rejected 25 transcripts about Hurricane Katrina since this past summer. On one hand, some of the writing was very good; however, as a publicist I can tell you right now that the Hurricane Katrina story has been covered, and I will not be able to get you any media coverage. Period. Pass. You can tell me that I am wrong (which I hear all of the time when I pass on something), but I feel the need to warn you. There are really shady publishing and publicity companies that will tell you what you want to hear and take your money and not care. They are lying to you. OK, I am done with my public service announcement for this book and will move on.

The main reason why I am co-authoring this book is because I am for "crap reduction." I want to educate authors on a changing industry as well as share useful information so they do not go into the publishing world in the dark. I have seen that many do and many end up with a low-quality product that I have to turn down as a publicist. Examples of self-published disasters include books with yellow pages and tons of misspelled words in spite of the fact this so-called publisher provided an editor that the author had to pay for. I have seen lack of professional photography, and the very worst problem of all is the book cover itself. Do you know the saying: "Don't judge a book by its cover?" I have an answer for you … the media will and if your book has any of the other above attributes, please do not call me or send me your product.

I am going to have return to public relations just for a minute. One of the saddest things I see is when people come to me with a crappy book they also told me they paid XYZ publisher thousands of dollars a month for zero-to-little coverage. The little coverage was usually an interview with the publishing house radio show. Not good. I have also seen expensive programs that will guarantee one article a month over a six-month period. I hope readers of this book will at the very least learn how to hire a good publicist. On the flipside of this coin, you have the authors who really think they do not need to hire a publicist and can market the book on their own. On one hand, this is good because at least they are not wasting their money on a bad publishing house that does not know what they are doing. However, if you do not market your book at all your book sales will come to a screeching halt. Don't get me started on the marketing professional who has a background in technology, but insists they can effectively market their book because they have a marketing degree. Here is one question for you: Do you specifically know the book segment producer at NBC national news or *The Today Show?* If the answer is "no," chances are you may need to hire somebody.

I really hope you enjoy the book; and in turn, it helps you make the right decision when selecting a publishing house. Most importantly, I hope this book saves you from publishing a piece of crap.

Michele (1L) Smith

VANITY CIRCUS

Chapter 1: The Good, the Bad and the Brutally Ugly

"I intend to put up with nothing that I can put down."
~ Edgar Allan Poe

Want to know a way to absolutely ruin an utterly brilliant day? Be forced to read a tragically written manuscript (fiction or non-fiction … doesn't matter). In our opinion, nothing is worse than being forced to read a manuscript that for all intents and purposes is drivel to the extreme — and perhaps the most pain we can possibly experience is also to be subjected to horrible, horrible dialog. Nothing makes a reader wince more than weak dialog written in a stilted and idiotic manner. We promise you that forcing a reader to strain through inane and meaningless dialog will drive them mad. So with that said, it's time to tell you about The Good, The Bad and The Brutally Ugly when it comes to sifting through and reading a pile of manuscripts.

The Good

The Good manuscript while it has a handful of weaknesses — a missing comma or perhaps a misplaced semi-colon — will make the reader smile, having now been enlightened and even delighted by the words. The Good always develop their story and characters and take their time to really think out what they're about to submit to an agent or publisher. The Good at least try to proof read their work, and therefore, minimize mistakes. The Good know they need an editor and proof reader and happily and graciously submit to the process with the understanding that it will make their work better. The Good also know they are not designers and do not attempt to draw their covers by hand or use a lame version or low-end design program in an attempt to present their ideas in tacky clip art. The Good submit to the idea that a graphic designer knows his or her job — and sit back and allow them to do it unimpeded without random notes about moving a line a little more to the .5-inch margin. The Good know they are writers and not publicists, and do not interfere or ask a dozen questions about why such and such magazine didn't review their books. They accept public relations as a process and go along for the ride. They show up on time for interviews and happily oblige their publicist with their schedules, so they don't miss any media opportunities due to an unexpected flight to China. We like The Good. They understand the value of 3L Publishing services and are a pleasure to work with.

The Bad

The Bad write marginally good stories or fiction books, but accept the fact it may not be perfect. The Bad do accept an editor's advice but only after arguing continuously over the use of words like "which" used in place of "that." The Bad also try and argue about the use of a professional editor at all and change back all the suggested changes in a mental tug of war that they eventually lose over the idea of, "It's my book not yours." The Bad also love to boss around the graphic designer — even though they have the artistic skills of a five-year-old. The Bad argue over every design and template, and always ask that we use Times New Roman as their font of choice, because, well, *it looks right.* The Bad fall in love with their horrible dialog and try to convince the editor why it's so darned good. The Bad also fall in love with their storyline and even defend their right to tell the ending at the beginning. The Bad want to choose their own printer, because they're cheaper. The Bad don't listen to reason when we plead with them not to interfere with the production process by calling our sales representative on their own without our permission — and then wonder where all the confusion came from. The Bad really secretly wish we would just go away and let them publish their book on their own — but they also know just enough to know better. The Bad don't need public relations — the book will sell itself. And if they do invest in public relations, they spend $500 on a press release they intend to pitch on their own with no awareness that the press will laugh at the writer as publicist and not take it seriously.

The Brutally Ugly

The Brutally Ugly insist their writing doesn't need an editor or proofer … period. The Brutally Ugly also explain that their manuscripts don't need an editor because their friend Daisy who is an English teacher at Pookipsie High School in Idaho said so. The Brutally Ugly argue when we insist they rename their book from *The Cabbage Patch Monster Rides Across America* — and it's not a kid's book. In fact, The Brutally Ugly name their book *Shattered Lives* and insist the name is original — even though we have 10 other submissions with that title. The Brutally Ugly believe they don't need a graphic designer either, and they can design their own covers, see and doesn't that clip art look awesome, dude! The Brutally Ugly also tell the whole story in the first line of the book; they don't develop the story; they have too many characters running around to know the difference; and their dialog sounds like two two-year-olds in deep conversation. The Brutally Ugly's work is, in fact, so bad that 3L Publishing can't even revive it with a trip to our friendly neighborhood writing coach. The Brutally Ugly tell us our company is "dubious" when we pass on their work and also tend to scream at us when we reject their manuscript by yelling, "I pass on you!" … sometimes even in Russian. We read one page of The Brutally Ugly's work and know where it goes — on the rejection pile.

4 VANITY CIRCUS

Chapter 2 – Why We Rejected "Shattered Lives" Part 10 … Or Rejection Hurts Both of Us

"The Guru has shattered the shackles on my feet, and has set me free."
~ Sir Guru Ganth Sahib

You're amped up and finished with what you genuinely believe is going to be a best-selling masterpiece sure to receive rave reviews in the *New York Times*. The only hesitation is you're a little uncertain about chapter one, "Hey it's not my best chapter in the book," you will eventually say to your prospective publisher should you be blessed enough to get him or her on the phone. Want to know what the acquisitions manager or reader thinks but probably won't say either on the phone or in writing, "What! Are you crazy?"

Smart Girls:

Carrie: What? Now? What about last night, all those concerns?
Big: Fuck it. You'll need material for the sequel.

~ Sex and the City

Rule number one when submitting a manuscript, always make chapter one the very best chapter in the book not the weakest. Why? Because the reader won't get past page one or even the end of the first chapter if it's poorly written, weak, boring or uninteresting. All authors absolutely must understand that publishers receive literally hundreds of thousands of manuscripts a year. You do not want your first impression to be your weakest work. It may even sound preposterous to many writers that anyone would dare to make such a ridiculous mistake; but you would be absolutely stunned how many authors "confess" that they feel chapter one is not their strongest chapter.

So the real deal (because we're always honest), you must remember when you pursue either traditional publishing or the New Publishing model, you cannot submit weak work. Publishers receive so many manuscripts and have so little time your manuscript won't make it past page one much less the last page of the chapter if the reader immediately senses yet another literary mess or "snooze-fest" coming their way. Readers may only spend a fraction of each day actually reading submissions. These days, readers are pulled in so many different directions and play so many roles in the company that an exercise in what turns into a painful experience of reading yet another horrible manuscript becomes torturous. When the reader even glances at the first paragraph and senses a dud their mind tunes out ... *have to pick up the groceries, don't forget to do the laundry* ... anything to distract them from yet another horrible book. You have to almost feel sorry for the reader responsible for sifting through a pile of junk as a part of their jobs — but then the really fantastic part comes when they finally stumble on that one really amazing fiction or non-fiction book. The one that they think, "Wow! I actually get paid to read this stuff."

We Do Judge a Book by Its Title

So what can you do as an author to prevent the reader from heavily sighing at the first sight, say, of your title? Number one, your title must rock, be original, catch their attention (in a good way); and convey a message of hope, intrigue, happiness or mystery. Your title should not embarrass the book buyer (e.g., 10 Ways to Commit Incest); deter the book buyer by not making them want to identify with the title that it is something they're interested in (e.g., I am Old and Ugly! How About You?); or come across as melodramatic drivel (e.g., Daisy's Dying Wish to Fall In Love with Prince Charming and Have Twins).

In 2009, 3L Publishing received a half-dozen manuscripts with the melodramatic title "Shattered Lives." First, had we not received so many "Shattered Lives," we might have shrugged off the title as perhaps just negative and melodramatic. Yet by the fourth book with that awful title, we began to not only turn it into a literary inside joke, but then wondered why? Why does anyone think that is a provocative and interesting title? It didn't make us feel hopeful, intrigued, happy or curious. It did make the writing immediately suspect as poorly written, because this now very unoriginal title graced the cover of six seemingly bad manuscripts that we had no interest in reading.

So your title creates the all-important first impression of your book. The importance of a catchy and interesting title plays just as an important of a role as the impression left by the first chapter. A hokey or just silly title can repel the reader and actually discourage them from cracking open page one. Please realize a significant difference exists between clever and creative titles and inane and stupid titles that make the reader groan. A clever title will provoke the reader to wonder: "Hmm … what could this be trying to say or suggest?" Even with this book, *Vanity Circus* is a clever metaphor for the chaos and craziness of the publishing and writing worlds. The reader is at once intrigued by its uniqueness and puzzled by its meaning yet between the two reactions, it promises to lure the reader into at least reading the back-cover copy versus quickly hitting the delete button or tossing the book back on the shelf.

Also, please don't fall prey to the idea that "sex sells," therefore I will make my title sexy or dirty or pornographic. Reader demographics show that women purchase the majority of books. You know that most women do not openly go out and purchase a copy of *Playgirl.* In fact, you also know that *Playgirl* magazine sales do not rival *Playboy* magazine sales. What does this tell you? It tells you that the majority of your reading audience (women) — the segment likely to make your book a best seller — will have little or no interest in purchasing a book titled, "Eat me! Ten Ways to Give and Receive Oral Pleasure."

Excuse Me! So Sorry, but Chapter One Sucks!

Now that we've given you the lowdown on titles, let's move back to a discussion about chapter one. Some people find it difficult to write a strong chapter one while other writers find it a challenge to write a strong ending. If you find chapter one your nemesis then it should move you to pay extra special attention to chapter one. Why? Because most likely your book will not be rejected based on a weak ending, but it will certainly find its way to the "no" pile based on a weak opening.

> "For those doubters, do this simple routine: take 10 pennies — count 'em one at a time. You'll note that you don't start with zero when counting that first penny. When you get to 10, you're ready for 10 more. This year of 2010, is our No. 10 penny, or, the "last year" of the first decade."
> ~ Morrow: Now Let's Get Some Pennies Out and Count to 10

Evaluations of chapter one fall under what we call "the rule of 10." No, it's not some scientific rule discovered by Einstein or apparently the rule to determine the beginning or ending of the decade. The rule of 10 suggests that most readers don't read past page 10 to decide whether or not your manuscript will pass go to the next level of evaluation. In a traditional publishing house, this exercise involves the reader giving your sample chapter a positive evaluation and pushing it up the line to the next level of approval, which is usually an acquisitions manager followed by a recommendation to the editor in chief who has the almighty power to green light the project and offer you a contract. Remember, (and we'll get to this later) new and mid-level authors don't receive advances anymore. The New Publishing model vets the manuscript in much the same way, so if you were hoping the new model might be your salvation, umm, no.

So the rule of 10 requires that your writing, concept, story or premise be so strong, so interesting that you move through the chain of command and toward a "yes." Truth in sales time here: Most readers really apply *the rule of one.* Any major blunders or obvious faux pas exposed on page one will send your manuscript packing and back through email with a big, fat no way. I know you want to think the best of the reader. "Oh, come on they have to go past page one, right?" Nope! Readers are busy, busy folks and can smell a stinky manuscript often by the first sentence. And we know this may sound unimaginable, but some writers actually pull the biggest blunder possible. They tell the whole story in the first line. No kidding true story. We had a beginning author submit a manuscript that said in the very first sentence: I die at the end. Not good all my writer friends. Not good. No intrigue here. I know *that* quickly that my hero kicks off by the end. What fun is that?

Chapter one from beginning to end shows the reader some critical information about your writing and story-telling abilities. That aforementioned first sentence should not reveal your story's end. In fact, it should have very little to do with how it ends. If the book you're submitting is a work of non-fiction then the first chapter should set up the sequential run of the book in an almost documentary style. What does that mean? Your non-fiction table of contents should be set up in a kind of building-blocks style. Each chapter builds and lends to the other. It makes sense. A non-fiction book usually sets up its thesis or premise, and then the supporting chapters provide the development and explanation of the thesis or premise — and guide the reader through something to persuade or sway them to understand, agree or acknowledge what you wrote makes sense.

On the other hand, chapter one in a piece of fiction establishes the essential framework for the story. It introduces the hero or protagonist. It provides the essence of the story; establishes the setting; and plants the seed of the plot. It may or may not introduce all of the players in the story; but at the very least it provides the launch pad for the story. It doesn't move so rapidly into the story as to not develop the essentials described above. It begins a slow build of all elements; fully explains motivation and character; and with supreme giftedness starts to gently pull the reader through the story.

A huge, huge mistake will often take root in chapter one. We call this the "impatient writer syndrome." The impatient writer so eager to tell his or her story will hurl the characters into place. Take no time to build and develop them. And within pages the impatient writer expects the reader to fully understand each and every character. This problem then gets exacerbated by dialog plagued by a two-pronged dilemma: dialog for each character sounds identical and dialog is bad.

The dialog itself can be very revealing of a poorly written manuscript. Dialog plays an artful part in great literature. It needs to sound natural and most importantly appropriate to the demographic of the character and time period.

Smart Girls:

"Now Daisy Duke why ain't you's sitting the way you's should?"

Sir Drakeley's butler enters the ornate room and stops.

"Sir, can I get you another bottle of vodka?"

"No, Daisy Duke ain't sittin' like she should."

"Yes, sir I see."

"Now you's make her sit now, would ya."

"Yes, sir you're the master of the house."

The butler sets down the tray and tries to force the Great Dane to sit. The dog stands firm.

As mentioned earlier, bad dialog can be compared to really bad food — it tastes and smells bad; therefore, I won't eat it. Bad dialog that sounds hokey, contrived or cliché grates on the reader's inner ear. It destroys suspension of disbelief. And just makes a potentially great story one that the reader easily passes on.

Bad dialog can be awful for many reasons, but the key reason may not stand out to the writer. The most obvious is stilted dialog inappropriate to the age group or time period of the characters. In other words, a 30-year-old woman in 1880 does not talk the same way as 12-year-old boys in 1970. Each character will have expressions and idioms unique to the cadence and inflection of their voices (as written). It's very difficult to illustrate really bad dialog; yet bad dialog can be the first in a series of disastrous red flags that kill your chance of being published. Before you even consider chapter one as finished, read your dialog aloud with some friends. We like to call the hokey dialog the part where you "grimace" because you just heard how awful what you wrote sounds.

Examples of dialog:

Bad: *Joe, a 60-year-old grandfather, says, "Dude! Let's catch a ride in my fucking truck. Cool dude."*

Good: *Joe, a 60-year-old grandfather, says, "Hey! I've got errands. Hop in my truck. Let's go."*

You see while the writing itself isn't bad, the age-appropriate response of a 60-year-old saying an expression commonly used by 20-year-old men sounds odd and inappropriate. You have Grandpa sounding like a surfer dude who wants to drive his "fucking truck." How many surfer grandfathers do you know? We'll bet on the side of not many. How does the reader react? "This writer doesn't know what she is doing." And if that idiotic dialog happens to be say on page one? Uh-oh! Here goes the "no" pile.

The Grammar Police

Now follow up this horrible dialog with the next errors: poor writing and weak grammar — and you've got winner, winner chicken dinner! Weak writing is almost like throwing chum to a swarm of hungry sharks. Our office joke involves calling some readers "grammar police." Grammar police, readers with degrees in English, love proper grammar — and they adore telling you when you goof up your grammar, syntax or style. Oh, grammar police are the snarkiest people. We personally try to avoid putting on our badges and pass weak writers through the process and encourage them to consider editing services. None the less, traditional publishers don't offer editorial services so all those readers with English degrees and penchants to tell everyone about their errors, will be turned off by your mistakes. In fact, if grammar isn't your forté, we strongly encourage you to hire a professional editor before you send your manuscript off for inspection. The grammar police won't act sympathetic to your misspelled words when you do have spelling and grammar checks on your word processor. Grammar police will see it as a sign of disrespect. So, we recommend you clean up your work before you submit it anywhere.

12 VANITY CIRCUS

Chapter 3: Book Covers that Rock or Suck!

"There are book to which the front and back covers are the best parts."
~ Charles Dickens

All smart girls have to admit — they love to look at pretty pictures. Come on. You like many others go to the bookstore only to stand and stare at book covers, as if this somehow tells you the contents are good, bad or decidedly ugly. We are a visual society. Why do you think comic books sell so well? We want to see pretty pictures to go with a side of words. So, book covers whether you like it or not often trumps words. Yes, the sad facts of life. So, if you happen to be one of those writers who firmly believes that *anyone* can draw a picture and slap it on a book, please take yourself outside to the woodshed — your po-po paddle awaits.

The book cover and the back-cover copy often play the most important roles in the buying decision. Watch book buyers browse in your local bookstore. What do they do? We can tell you with almost 100-percent accuracy. They walk up the closest table. Glance at the array of book titles, stare at the cover, find something that intrigues them, pick it up, and read the back cover copy. They like what they see *and* read — bam! Sale made. Now this scenario excludes the motivated buyer. Who is the motivated buyer? The one on a mission to purchase a book he or she heard or read about in a magazine or on television (and we'll cover that in the chapter on publicity). The motivated buyer walks into the bookstore and goes straight for your book — so cover is not quite as important.

The rest of the shoppers, we'll call casual browsers, do care very much about your book cover and title. Some people will actually pick a book up just because of the cover. They don't even look at the title. They just like the pretty picture. I know, I know it sounds so prosaic. Are we all so simple? Well, the majority of us are. So go with the majority rule if you want a best seller. If you don't care then please go right ahead, take out your crayons, and knock yourself out. More serious writers, please put down the felt-tip pens and listen up. Please take the oath of good art: *I swear to not try and draw my own book cover ever, ever, ever.* Now this oath only applies to self-publishers. The rest of you are "covered" (yuck, yuck). Traditional publishers will supply the artwork for you (not always as good as one would assume), and here at 3L Publishing, we only use professional graphic and fine artists for covers and illustrations. No drawing and coloring allowed unless you're one of our children who wants to draw at his or her little desk near our own — that is fine.

You have several different types of cover treatments to choose from, including photographs with text treatments, fine art with text treatments, and straight-up text treatments. Please never, ever use clip art … again we need another oath: *I swear never, ever to use tacky clip art for my book cover.* We can't describe all of the submissions we receive where the author attempted to be an artist and includes some bad piece of clip-art for the cover "suggestion." What a mega turnoff on the scale of beyond turnoff. We scowl — the wrinkles even show through our Botox — at the very sight of some awful clip-art cover. Just don't go there. And if you've already done it, and your finger is centimeters from "send" to info@3LPublishing.com, please don't do it. It just immediately distracts from your perhaps great writing.

Here is your super-duper tip for the day: Don't use anything but a cover page! How's that … no time wasted on your doodles gone wrong. Just put the book's title, subtitle, name, and copyright with All Rights Reserved. Voile! Imagine how simple. No muss, fuss or mess.

Treatment … Not Sewage Treatment

As we mentioned, you have three cover choices, including photograph, art or text treatments. We recommend when the author is reasonably attractive (although we will not specifically cite a case of the "uglies" as a reason we don't want you photographed) and the book's content is driven by personality that the author appear on their book's cover. Author photos work very well for certain non-fiction books, true stories, biography, autobiography or memoir.

Author photos look misplaced and odd when used for fiction or just because the publisher couldn't think of something appropriate. We also have to suggest a photographer who has excellent airbrushing skills for older authors. Sorry, vanity, vanity, vanity — it applies when your face is going to appear on thousands of copies. Do you really want to look terrible? Probably not. And here is something to get some people's hackles up. Go for Botox. It works! Oh, now if you're a naturalist, please don't write us letters and tell us how bad we are. Let's just get real now. Women and men of a certain age can definitely benefit from a little Botox. We quit trying to be subtle about it. Just enjoy yourself. And don't do it again if it really bothers your sensibilities.

If your book is a work of fiction then graphic art or illustration works best. A photo of a specific person used on a work of fiction can be somewhat misleading. People might construe it as a true story — although once your work of fiction becomes a movie, it's cool to have the actor's images used on the cover vs. an illustration. Or if you use the back of some unknown person, that works well too. Beautiful illustrations turn a casual book into a piece of art to adorn one's bookshelf. Our forthcoming book titled *The Feast at the Beach* by William Louis Widmaier has a stunning watercolor image on it. An author could not ask for anything more than to have her book out on display on someone's coffee table or bookshelf simply because the book cover image is so stunning. Now remember, an ugly image works in reverse — a creepy, horrible or just ugly cover incites the reader to hide your book from sight.

Also, keep the image relevant to the content or at least intriguing. You do not want the image to mislead the reader that your book about eating and France is about hot women in bikinis. No! While a few men will pick up the book expecting a sexy, Girls-Gone-Wild read, your true audience will avoid the book. So, make sure the cover doesn't create great expectations and turn off your prospective reader. Now if you can work the women in hot bikinis into your fabulous beach book about skinny-dipping in the South of France, fine. Just keep it tasteful and keep their suits on.

Speaking of taste ... Okay, not everyone defines good taste the same; but we can assure you certain standards of decency exist. Don't push it. We don't care if you wrote a romance book or erotica. Keep your cover tasteful, decent and attractive. You don't need to publish what could be construed as pornography. The bookstores will not carry it out front and will possibly shove it in an adult section. Your name will be associated with porn ... not good friends. Not if you intend to be a serious-minded writer.

And finally, a great book cover can be created from just a fabulous text treatment. The title treatment can become the entire cover — and work very well. Emphasis on font sizes and how the letters merge or the font type and colors can create a true masterpiece. So, don't always assume an image will be the most effective approach. So many different text treatment exist to contrast and play with fonts and colors. Just go out and look at what some graphic artist came up using just text alone as her artistic tool. And one more thing, white space can be artfully messed with too. White space if applied right can emphasize words or even images in a way that puts things on or off balance or even in balance. One of these days, 3L will bring out just a text-based cover. We really like to push these boundaries. It's fun and eye pleasing for the average reader.

One thing is for certain, do not approve or have created a cover where the viewer inexplicably asks, "What is that thing?" Bad sign. Your cover above all else must communicate its title and sub-title in an easy-to-read and understandable format. Readers should not pick up your book, frown and toss it back out of sheer misunderstanding of what it looks like and says. A toss back in the pile is not good for sales.

Chapter 4: The Book as Platform – A Winning Outlook on Publishing

"The free-lance writer is the person who is paid per piece or per word or perhaps."
~ *Robert Benchley*

We constantly educate our authors about how their book is not a singular, passive revenue stream. We inform them how their book can become a business with multiple revenue streams. When our clients come to us with such tunnel vision, we explain the "business-in-a-box" model and slowly light up the tunnel until, "ta-da," the realization of a business opportunity hits them smack on the side of the head. They finally understand the concept, and then they run with it. When you write a book, it is a platform and opportunity to do many other things such as speaking engagements, workshops, and increase current business activities.

Did someone just give me a microphone?

When *SMASH: a Smart Girl's Guide to Marketing and Public Relations* first came out last year, we were immediately flooded with speaking opportunities. We were surprised that people asked us to speak without having read the book. When you publish a book, you are automatically viewed as

Smart Girls:

"The answer is out there, Neo, and it's looking for you, and it will find you if you want it to."
~ Trinity, The Matrix

an expert. Between the two of us, we do have the marketing and publishing experience to warrant the "expert" status, but to receive opportunities without even trying was pretty amazing. We were awestruck.

There are several ways to leverage this aspect of the "business-in-the-box" model. You can do what we did and take your stand-up comedy routine on the road. First, you will be asked to start with non-paid speaking engagements that you will need to start building your speaking resume. Now, you may be asking yourself, "Why would I want to do something for free?" Well, for one thing you may not be paid, but you will be able to sell your book at the back of the room. We have personally watched some of our authors speak and sell not one, but two or even four books to each person in the room. Second, by speaking in general you promote your core business. If you do not sell a book to everyone in the room you are still doing a 30- to 60-minute business promo to every person in that room. The exposure is priceless — and these people might turn into several new contracts for your core business.

Once you have built up a resume with the small guys, it is time to leverage this experience with major conferences that are related to your book or business. One very important question to ask your publicist is to find out if they will create pitch letters for you, and if they can submit them as well. When you are on a major conference circuit you are looking at 5K or 10K or even 50K for any speaking opportunity where you keynote. This is not bad income for the time spent — and most major conferences will cover travel as well. Oh, and P.S. you can write off your trip too. Last, when you speak to a group this large you know your Amazon sales are going to blow up. And, you will be famous. Ah, fame. Aren't we a culture full of fame-seekers? Yes, it seems so.

We need to get real for a minute because some people suck the big one when it comes to public speaking. We have seen some pretty bad speakers — and two in particular ended up in our screenplay *C-ASS*. Terrible speakers usually exhibit one of the following qualities: crappy content/lack of audience entertainment/interest/involvement/nervousness.

There is absolutely nothing wrong with being nervous when it comes to public speaking. Now, if you have a deathly fear of it you might *not* want to pursue

 **Smart Girls:**

"According to most studies, people's number one fear is public speaking. Number two is death. Death is number two. Does that sound right? This means to the average person, if you go to a funeral, you're better off in the casket than doing the eulogy."
~ Jerry Seinfeld

this aspect of your "business-in-a-box" model. However, if your fear is minor and you can correct it with a class (or even a nice glass of Merlot) or start attending a group like Toastmasters ... go for it.

Most people, unless they are a born entertainer feel nervous when they start a presentation until they get to know their audience. Once they are in for a couple minutes the nerves subside, and they actually enjoy the experience. Most people enjoy themselves because they are talking about a topic they feel passionate about; therefore, the speaking engagement becomes fun. Isn't that a novel concept? On the flipside, there is nothing wrong with not wanting to speak if you truly feel uncomfortable. If you are forced to do something you do not want to do your nerves will cause you to do silly things like blurt out things you do not mean; ask for everyone's opinion in the room for buy in; and overall make your entire audience uncomfortable while they have one single thought going through their heads, *"Please God, make it stop."*

 **Smart Girls:**

"There are three things to aim at in public speaking: first, to get into your subject, then to get your subject into yourself, and lastly, to get your subject into the heart of your audience."
~ Alexander Gregg

Before you decide to get in front of the microphone you should carefully contemplate content, your audience and interest factor. Over the last year, we have seen more horrific speakers at various networking events than we wish to remember. Most of the time, they are walking, talking infomercials, and occasionally we leave wondering what the f*** was that about? When we are really scratching our heads that hard about something despite the horrible content, the entertainment factor had to have made up for it. First, make sure you are passionate about your content and look at what takeaways your audience should get out of your performance. I know, I know, you are thinking but what's in it for me? I just want to talk about my upcoming seminar. See, now you're being an infomercial. It is best to stick to helpful, relative or inspirational information where you have your audience *engaged.* The engaged part is key, because once you have them hooked you will have followers (and possibly stalkers) for life. Last, please do your audience a favor and *be interesting.* If you are boring everyone in the room — and you see them leaving your snooze-fest — chances are public speaking may not be for you. The worst part you may not have considered is the speaking paradox. What can blow up your business to great success can also destroy it on a level of a bomb exploded in the middle of your office. As much as word gets around about positive speaking experiences even more word gets around (well, more like snickered and gossiped about) about bad speaking experiences. Don't become the brunt of our jokes! *Seriously!* If you can't speak, go to Toastmasters and learn how.

Workshops and Seminars ... Oh, Boy!

Once you are published, your book will be a great platform to launch workshops and seminars. Workshops and seminars can be done both online as well as in person, and not only will you generate book sales you will be *charging* for workshop/seminar attendance as well. What a *novel* idea!

"I'm conducting a seminar on multiple personality disorders, and it takes me forever to fill out the name tags."
~ Unknown

In an ideal world, you should start working on content for these while your book is at the printer. The content for the book will obviously be done, but you need to figure out how you can turn your book into a workshop, and what physical takeaway or written plan your attendees will receive. When you have ironed out these *little* details you also need to figure out how to market your events. We have to share with you that if you do not market your events, no one is going to show up. It also does not feel good to have no one show up at your book-launch party either. Isn't that your worst nightmare kind of like that bad dream where you find yourself in the middle of a crowd with just your underwear ... doesn't make you feel all warm and fuzzy does it?

There are some great marketing tools online, and your publicist should be aware ... if not fire the person. One of our favorite ways to promote our events is through MeetUp. MeetUp is a great, inexpensive online group service you can sign up for to create your meeting group and market your events. The best part of MeetUp is that once your page is up, MeetUp invites everyone in the system interested in your particular topic. MeetUp also accepts payments, which is pretty cool, right?

Another great way to promote your events is through LinkedIn. We have to warn you about LinkedIn though. In the interest groups we belong to, there seems to be a lot of cranky people with free time on their hands that are ready to mudsling at any time. Our recommendations are to test the water, find an interest group that is a good fit, participate *first,* and then promote.

Last, we started out this chapter talking about how your book is going to be a platform for your business itself. We can guarantee you that if you own an auto body shop and you write a book on a Smart Girl's Guide to fixing your car ... you are going to get business from local women simply because you have a book out. If you are reading this and are wondering if this is you, yes ... we are talking about you.

Chapter 5: Self Publishing, Vanity Press or Do-It-Yourself-ers

"Vanity is my favorite sin." ~ Al Pacino

Self publishing, publish on demand, traditional, and now New Publishing … Publishers everywhere and so many choices what's a writer to do? Before you get all quivering and quaking with fear and a need to pop a Xanax to calm your nerves, keep reading. We want to help alleviate a quick trip to the pharmacy to consume anti-depressants to manage your publishing anxiety. First, like the warning label on any good prescription bottle or Diet Coke can, we want to not just warn you, but beg you to educate yourself before you sign on the line of any contracts you may have placed in front of you. And this may be hard to control yourself too. Any time a so-called publisher or someone with the title of publisher calls and says they want to publish your manuscript, refrain from the happy dance just yet.

Our sad cautionary tale comes from a 95-year-old World War II veteran we'll call Stew. Poor Stew searched for the perfect publisher of his war stories and found one. So grateful and pleased to have his legacy in print, he signed — and he signed away all of his rights to future work to that same publisher. The unscrupulous publisher didn't deliver on a single promise — yet they still have "first right of refusal" on any piece of literature the poor old guy produces. He sadly shows up at 3L and wants us to publish his new book, which was very good. Unfortunately, when he reported his contractual obligation with the first publisher we were forced to turn him away. This sad story is common — and please don't let it be you who comes begging for assistance after being swindled out of your literary "rights."

Now that said, you may be tempted more than ever to toss in the towel and just self publish. Well, we have some information to share about self publishing. Before we launch into it, we're going to stray to a Smart Girl's technique, which is to give you The Good, The Bad and The Brutally Ugly, because self publishing deserves its own special treatment in this respect.

The Good

The self publisher knows without question that she is a writer not an editor or graphic designer. She writes her book and then hires an editor to clean it up and eliminate typos, style and grammar errors, and anything questionable content-wise. She then researches and finds a talented graphic artist and does not sit down and attempt to draw stick figures. The Good relies on her graphic artist to do her job and follow a bona-fide template for the book's interior design. The Good doesn't try and purchase a copy of InDesign and attempt the impossible — learn a program that takes years of experience and skill to use. The Good does take her professionally edited and designed manuscript to a reputable printer and has a perfect-bound book created. The Good doesn't attempt to do her own PR and does hire a proper publicist who will do everything possible to avoid letting anyone know the book was self published. The Good has a professionally designed website created for her and leverages her writing talent to blog and support her book. She also has the PR expert write the media kit and fully understands it's not a good idea to attempt to do this without help. The Good also understands that because she self published her chances of getting national distribution are next to nil — but that's OK. She is really only using her book to get speaking gigs and help grow her primary business, which involves seminars and workshops — all based, of course, on her self-published book that now people "oooh" and "aaahhh" over, because she did such a good job.

The Bad

The bad don't believe they need an editor — heck I'll just do it myself. The Bad don't have any training in editing, and don't know anything about style. "Style? What style?" They just figure they can save money, because, "Hell, I know how to use a period." The Bad also go out and purchase a copy of

InDesign and start trying to use it. After much cursing and frustration, they toss it out and figure, "Well, then what's a word processor for anyway? I'll just make me a Microsoft template." The Bad then shrink the margins in an attempt to create the correct format. The Bad then simply put words in place of a cover, call around to find a few printers, find one, and soon realize they don't get it when the printer asks, "What size template do you want?" They don't know how to resize it anyway and take it down to the printer to have the printer's $10 an hour designer slap it into a pre-made template for printing. The Bad then get their book off press — no design, spelling and grammar errors and all. They look around, call Grandma and cry, "Hey there Granny, $12 bucks get you my book." Granny buys it, forces her friends to buy it, and coerces the rest of the family to buy lest she cut them out of her will. The writer makes $50 for sales to reluctant family members and ends up with 2,000 copies all sitting, gathering dust in the shed.

The Brutally Ugly

The Brutally Ugly didn't pass high school English. In fact, the Brutally Ugly really don't like to write — but want to be famous for something ... anything. The Brutally Ugly write their memoir about their first trip to the North Carolina pig farm — and how they fell in love with a pink sow named Wanda, but Wanda got slaughtered. They cried for weeks and then decided to write a book on cruelty to animals and "screw bacon" pass me the ham. They attempt to illustrate their book with hand-drawn pictures of Wanda and use red crayon to show off the slaughter techniques. They take drawings and printouts to Kinko's and make an original copy that they then have Joe Bob behind the counter create 100 copies of their masterpiece, "Don't Kill Wanda!" for $30 each copy. They get "Don't Kill Wanda," and think, "What a beautiful book. Now I'm famous." They try to sell copies to PETA, but PETA turns them down and muses over the hand-drawn pictures, laughing the whole time. They try to sell it to their family members and eventually their mother purchases a copy just so she can tell everyone her daughter is a published author ... "See! I'm so proud." And even though they should throw away this piece of junk, they drag it out every Christmas to show their grandchildren that, "Look your Aunt wrote a book." The smaller children cry when they see the slaughter drawings and the older children think their aunt is really weird.

You're so Vain You Probably Think this Book is about You

So the reality of self publishing can get really ugly, which is why we started saying, "Lift a rock find a writer." We joke about that all the time. Some may find it offensive; but you will not find it offensive when you find yourself putting $29.99 on the counter to purchase what turns into an agonizing reading adventure into a book filled with typos, grammar errors, and little to no coherent intellectual reasoning or sound story structure. "How can this be?" You wonder as you flip to the last page to read the bio. You soon realize the book was published by a little-known press called Bear Skin Leather Co. Where are they located? In a little town called Patterson, Calif. You grow suspicious. I didn't know there was a publisher in Patterson? You scratch your head, and then do a Google search. Nope, no website either. Here is the real deal: You just got cheated out of $29.99 by Bob who printed the book under a self-made publishing house that is no more than his basement. Welcome to vanity press, a place where all humans on the planet with no training can write their life stories even if they were raised on a potato farm in Idaho and have absolutely nothing meaningful to say except: "Well them there 'taters' ... they taste great."

Vanity press became a more popular publishing method after the computer and digital printing brought the costs down to a level that the average person could afford. The advent of new publishing technology brought on a tidal wave of some good, but mostly bad books to flood the market. Many want-to-be authors got it into their minds that they could surly become millionaires by publishing their own books — no experience necessary, but a lot of moxie and enthusiasm to be able to say, "I wrote a book." Many of these authors also approached overseas publishers that will produce even cheaper books — all for a great package price. Yes, they produce books alright — did we mention that "crap" problem? Yes, I think we did. So yes in today's world anyone can publish a book — but not necessarily a good book.

Looks Like a Pig, Quacks Like a Duck

Smart Girls:

Avoid the stigma of self publishing. We want your money not your book.

Now we're giving vanity press a bad rap. Reality is that vanity press — while it opens the market to everyone who has a book idea — can work for some (depends on what you're going to do with the book) and not for others. You can purchase editorial and graphic services and create your own custom publication — and that is how it will be viewed by the media. It is very difficult to overcome set ideas about vanity press with the media too.

Why do you suppose that is when not all self-published books are bad? Well, who works predominantly for the print media in particular? Writers ... ding, ding, ding. You got it. And most writers often can spot your weak writing from a mere glance. The other thing you should know. Writers can be a contentious crowd. If they can't overcome the hurdles presented by a traditional publisher your attempt at writing what in their minds looks like amateur hour ultimately pushes buttons. All one has to do is hang out in a few writer's groups and watch the jealousy and tantrums start. The book reviewers will see a homemade tome — and without flipping open a page throw it in their "special" file.

Why do so many folks have set ideas about vanity press? Back to the real professionals who know their stuff. Let's say you've sent your custom publication to an editor. One thing you need to know. Editors read piles and piles of submissions and press releases. They can spot the good from the bad. They live with deadlines. If you have not gone that extra mile to attempt to put your perhaps well-written book into a traditional, perfect-bound format it most likely will come in a spiral binding ... or worse stapled together. What message does that send? Oh, I know. Cheap, amateur and lame ... seriously I know you may not want to hear this information; but it is the editor's super secret thoughts. How do we know? Michelle (2L) was a professional editor for 10 years. She read and saw it all. And as much as it frustrates vanity-press fans

Smart Girls:

The Dude: These are, uh...
Brandt: Oh, those are Mr. Lebowski's children, so to speak.
The Dude: Different mothers, huh?
Brandt: No.
The Dude: Racially he's pretty cool?
Brandt: [laughs] They're not literally his children. They're the Little Lebowski Urban Achievers — inner city children of promise but without the necessary means for a — necessary means for a higher education. So Mr. Lebowski is committed to sending all of them to college.
~ The Big Lebowski

to hear this information: We all naturally make assumptions — especially when pressed for time. The natural assumption when one sees a spiral-bound book is it's not good. So strike one.

The Big Book of Lebowski

Now to be fair, vanity press can work quite well if you intend to use your book as a product to do back-of-the-room sales. Back-of-the-room sales may also help alleviate the spiral-binding problem. Now you can actually use the spiral-binding "perception" to leverage and increase sales. How's that you wonder? Buyers now know this book is a custom job. What do all custom jobs cost? More money than mass-produced books, and oh so that $39.99 price tag on this custom job written by hopefully the girl who just gave an amazing talk on her subject of expertise costs more. OK, as a consumer I can accept the extra price. Now you have an actual reason to do a limited print run and charge more on a custom project. Just realize that wasting money and sending it to the local book reviewer will not fool them.

Smart Self Publishers Win

The real lesson is to be strategic in why you intend to self publish. You can make the self-publishing model work in your favor if you have a strategy behind it. If you're going to use a self-published book as a giveaway at seminars and workshops or as a handout, that is good. People will perceive the value of this kind of publication and appreciate the spirit in which it is given and used.

A typo in a self-published book used in this nature gets forgiven. The grammar police put away their rifles and guns. And you can sell it for top dollar — as we said people know it costs more to produce and respect the extra cost.

On the flipside, self publishing a book and trying to make it masquerade as a book published by a traditional publishing house — and it is chockfull of errors and generally looks cheap and tacky — continues to create a fog of doubt. Yes, self-published books exist that are well-done, but these books are largely in the minority. We can stand 10 feet back from a self-published book and know it came off a self-publisher's press, which isn't necessarily a bad press; but an air of "something's not right" looms over these self-published books and gives it away. To the less-seasoned eye it might seem to blend right in with the others; but the ones in the know like the media and book reviewers — well, they always know. And the self-published book, which may we add probably cost a lot if you had it perfect bound, loses credibility and will not be given proper respect, reviews or accolades — all needed to help it reach a mass audience.

The real question becomes, why are you self publishing in the first place? Are you fed up with traditional publishing and want your book faster than 18 months (see chapter on traditional publishing)? Are you afraid your writing will be deemed unfit to publish so you are trying alternatives? Or are you using your book to support your business and have no expectation that it will be a best-seller? No matter what is the reason you've chosen to self publish, the rule for success requires you not eschew important professional help like an editor or graphic designer. Maybe your self-published book is a prize winner in the making. Good for you. Maybe you have friends at a major distributor who will help get it distributed as an independent book, and you want to keep 100 percent of your royalties. OK, sounds reasonable to us; but chances are you have none of the advantages. Statistics show that most self-published books sell no more than 50-100 copies — hardly enough to make it a best seller and generate any significant profits. So before you spend upward of $5,000 to $10,000 to wind up with 2,000 copies of a book that may never see the light of a Borders book shelf, consider your options carefully and keep reading.

Chapter 6: Traditional Publishing: "Oh Toto! We're not in Kansas anymore."

*"There are three rules for writing the novel.
Unfortunately, no one knows what they are."
~ W. Somerset Maugham*

Once upon a time, little Cathy writer published a book. She was all excited. "Wow," she thought, "I'm going to be rich and famous!" One day her editor called her and said, "Hey Cathy, your books are moving. Have you thought about hiring a publicist?" "A publicist? OK, where do I start?" "Try Jones and Peterson Agency." So little Cathy writer called the agency and quickly found out that without a $5,000 a month retainer she was out of luck. "Oh well … I guess the book will be fine, and once I get my first royalty check I can pay that price … Oh, but I will owe my agent 15 percent of my 8-12 percent. No worries. I'm going to be a best seller." Then one day about 18 months later, little Cathy received her royalty check! "Wow," she thought, "I'm rich now!" She opened it with glee and anticipation of the new mansion and Mercedes she was sure she could now afford. She did a double-take: $56.95.

Little Cathy couldn't afford a publicist much less a trip to McDonalds. How did this happen? In traditional publishing or even using overseas services where they sell your self-published tome for you, the return on investment (ROI) or royalties rarely pay off in big checks you can take and make a down payment on a Mercedes or even afford a publicist. Had little Cathy taken her publisher's advice and procured a publicist her sales might have escalated; but the sad truth lies in the math.

Let's just say that little Cathy finally sold 50,000 books (which is a nice figure for a book that sells well), and it retails for $15 and made $750,000; she received 10 percent in royalties at $75,000; her agent got 10 percent of that amount at $7,500; she spent $5,000 a month on public relations for six months, which cost $30,000. Now she has paid out $37,500; Take her original $75,000 - $37,500 = $37,500. She made $37,500 for a book that took her at least six months to a year to write. Now consider that most books don't sell 50,000 copies but more like 3,000 copies — especially if the author doesn't do public relations work and get proper exposure. The money little Cathy just made doesn't include any buy backs that the publisher will do when the book stores send the leftover books back.

How do we know our figures are accurate? Check out this letter 3L Publishing received from an interested author.

Dear 3L Publishing,
I would like to share the following information with you regarding traditional royalty structure. My agent gets 15% of this which is .13455. My net royalty on each book is .76 cents. It will take selling 6689 books (@ .897) before I pay back the $6000 advance (of which my agent took 15% so my net advance was just $5100).
They also are charging me for their people doing the index in the back as per my contract — I'm not sure what that amount is. I don't know what this first print run is but it can't be much more than 50K books. If I sell 50,000 books I will net $38,000.00 which includes the advance. Deduct what I've spent on my own marketing from this amount — I hate to think what hourly wage this would come out to.
Foreign sales and other contingencies the publisher takes more. I hope this was helpful.
~ Anonymous

We are going to start with the basics here, in case there are some of you just starting to explore the mess that is traditional publishing. Oops ... I meant option, not mess. Examples of traditional publishing include the major publishing houses on New York row and are commonly pretty big operations such as Random House, Penguin, Harper-Collins as well as many others. The biggest pro for working with a traditional publisher is that your book will receive national distribution. National distribution is great. This means your book will be sold nationally in the major retail chains: Borders, Barnes and Noble, Target, Wal-Mart as well as several independent stores. There are some distributors that will even take your book overseas, and there is nothing in the world like receiving an email from some dude in Wales quoting your manuscript.

Now with the good, there are several things that are a little broken with the traditional system that we will painfully inform you about. First, let's talk about the bottom line or your ROI.

Yo! Where's My Money, Bi***?

Smart Girls:

"Ever notice how it's a penny for your thoughts, yet you put in your two-cents? Someone is making a penny on the deal!"
~ Steven Wright

We are going to be *really* honest here. Unless you are a former president of the United States, an A-List movie star (a la Brad Pitt or Oprah) you are not going to get an advance. Please, please, please stop deluding yourselves. If you happen to catch the episode of *My Life on The D List* where Kathy Griffin goes into her publisher expecting an advance then you know that even now someone as well known as Griffin doesn't get an advance.

Another pro with working with a traditional house is that you will not have to put in upfront costs for the production of your book. You will also be able to leverage a major publishing house's brand and the cache of having big name house on the spine of your book. We don't want to marginalize being associated with the value of a big 100-year-old name. Big name or not though you will not necessarily have the resources of the publishing house's marketing department past initial design and production, which is not to say they won't give you some support — but when we say *some* what we

> **Smart Girls:**
> "The beauty about the D-list is that people who are on it probably don't know they are."
> ~ Kathy Griffin

really mean is very little. They will measure expenditure of their resources with the simple phrase: What's in it for us?

So, without a name like J.K. Rowling, who by the way was largely ignored by major publishers when she tried to peddle Harry Potter, was living on public assistance when she finally got the attention of a publisher. An author the likes of J.K. Rowling has her publisher's full attention and has millions of dollars now at her disposal to do whatever she wants marketing-wise; but when you share the same publisher as Ms. Rowling and you have the book in town with no proven track record, where do you think those marketing dollars get invested?

So you will have to hire a publicist regardless. If you think you do not need to market your own book, please do the following: close this book and slap yourself on the head with it. Better? Please continue reading.

A Pain in My Pocketbook

From a royalty standpoint, you will earn between 8-12 percent of your retail price per book. This does not include the cut you need to pay for your agent. Also, if your books are not selling on the shelves you will be forced to purchase them back. Is this sounding a little bit backward yet?

We know you need to take into account the different offers that are out there, but all these negatives combined made us think, "Wow, that kind of sucks." We are positive that if you are Stephen King or Dean Koontz who cares; but for your average writer just trying to break into the industry. Ouch. Please look at your ROI in any offer you receive.

> **Smart Girls:**
> My retail cost minus 60 percent to publisher minus 15 percent to my agent = my take per book. *What?!*

We are now going to give you an idea of timing to receive the book

Smart Girls:

"Time. Time. Time. See what's become of me."
~ Hazy Shade of Winter, The Bangles

and timing to receive the above big fat ROI. Typically, it will take 18 months from signing a contract with a traditional publisher to have your book produced and on the shelves. Once this has occurred, you will wait another 12 to 18 months to receive your first royalty check. We are unfortunately not kidding around here, but hey ... if you are Sarah Palin who cares, right?

What happened? Is this really my book?

Now here comes the super lame part of traditional publishing. The measly royalties combined with the lack of upfront costs don't really make up for — at least not in our minds — what we're going to tell you about control and copyright. So here comes the true bad news: We can tell you with absolute assurance that once a traditional publishing house acquires your manuscript this is exactly what they do — *acquire your manuscript.*

The second you sign a contract you have just given the traditional publishing house the authority to butcher your manuscript without any input from you. In fact, by the time they are finished with your manuscript it might be as foreign to your body and as sickening as H1N1. Not kidding. If you think you own the copyright to your work when the publisher put their cash on the table and paid you money to acquire your work, umm, rude awakening time. You do not own your copyright anymore. Smaller boutiques may allow copyright retention upon completion of payment, but not in the traditional model. We really cannot think of anything more depressing especially as a writer. You pour in your blood, sweat and tears only to get butchered — and then you do not own your own manuscript — and at this point maybe you do not want to.

And how will you feel when your manuscript comes out as a beautiful book that you no longer own copyright on? Let's use 2L's screenplay experience. 2L had sold two screenplays years ago in the late 1990's. In 2L's case her well-written screenplay titled *Paris* eventually got renamed *Virtual Seduction,* which first aired on Showtime in 1996. After one of her characters was caught using the infamous "C" word in one scene, 2L learned the all-time hard way that once you sell your beloved project to an outside agent, the "C" word can be liberally used by people with a taste for profanity all to their heart's desire — that and your ending can be completely rewritten into some odd-ball conclusion that doesn't remotely resemble what you originally wrote. And when your work gets trashed by reviewers, which is inevitable when the director tries his hand at rewriting your script (and he's no writer), you are to your utter misery given "full" credit good, bad or brutally ugly. Who-hoo ... sign me up!

Now let's illustrate our point with little Cathy's original manuscript, which was about *10 Ways to Make Money on the Internet*. When the editor got a hold of little Cathy's book, she decided it should also include information on porno sites, which made Cathy really uncomfortable as a devout Christian. When little Cathy objected, the publisher reminded her she signed a contract that specifically gave her zero rights to approve final content or the cover for that matter. Not wanting a lawsuit on her hands little Cathy complied.

> *Smart Girls:*
> "Mommy, what *happened?*"
> ~ Dylan Smith, Age 2.

When the final draft was Fed-Xed to her little Cathy was horrified. They had changed the title to *10 Ways to Make Money on the Internet Selling Porn*. And devout Christian Cathy quickly hid the book. She could never show her friends and family. She had lost complete control over the title and content. She had no idea this would even happen. Truth is when you sign a contract with a publisher and don't address issues of title or content control, you can protest until you're out of breath and panting from exhaustion. It will do you no good. The publisher has billions of dollars and lots of money they can spend to legally

> *Smart Girls:*
> "Many a small thing has been made large by the right kind of advertising."
> ~ Mark Twain

make a case that ultimately says, "Too bad. You signed a contract. Now scoot and don't bother us!"

We once sat in a meeting mixed with 3L authors and authors who have gone the route of traditional publishing. The other authors all agreed that "most authors" don't like their book covers. The 3L authors looked perplexed. We *love* our book covers! Ah, we'll get into why that is in the next chapter.

Market. Market. Market.

We have more bad news for the traditional publishing clients. You will be on your own for marketing, and as we explained earlier you will need to hire your own publicist. Publicists at the very low end start at $3,000 per month. You will also need some very specific marketing tools such as a website with shopping cart, a media kit and any collateral to promote your signings/events. The traditional publishing houses do not provide these services, and you will be on your own. Last, please keep in mind that you will have a limited number of personal books to sell too so you will want to wisely spend money on marketing.

Customer service? What customer service?

Please keep in mind that with large houses you are one client out of thousands — and you are not going to get any special attention unless you are Barbara Walters. Also, when large publishers gobble up the small ones you can typically expect to get different representatives each time, and the various departments will not be on the same page, which can get pretty frustrating when you are trying to find out the status on your contract or if you are trying to find out the release date for your book. Most boutique firms will have a 24-hour return contact policy — and you should not expect this type of turnaround with the large firms.

So, we hope you learned something about traditional publishing after reading this chapter and hope this will give you a realistic view of how their model operates.

Chapter 7: Hybrid Publishers: Breaking all the Rules and Loving It

"He has, indeed, done it very well; but it is a foolish thing well done."
~ Dr. Samuel Johnson

Now that we've described self publishing and traditional publishing, you may feel completely discouraged. What is the point of being an author if you're going to make less than a burger flipper? In this fast-food business, you aren't *lovin' it, having it your way, or getting the beef* you want so what is a writer to do? Well, we do have some great news. The New Publishing or what we call the "Hybrid Model" may be the answer.

> **Smart Girls:**
> This isn't Burger King — You Can't have it your way.
> ~ Bumper sticker

Like so many authors we've met, we didn't want to self publish or jump through traditional publishing hoops only to end up a pauper having to tap dance for her food (although 1L can tap dance … and did so once on stage when 2L dared her). So we began really thinking about the industry and asking some important questions. The first one: Why do we have to publish books a particular way? Who made up these rules anyway? In the traditional publishing world, the so-called rules got made up with the advent of the printing press. OK, so they're still working off of 200-year-old rules, well, that makes perfect sense in the 21st century, right? And the self publishers … did anyone really think that model through?

Or did they just go, "Hey Skippy, we got us a press, ink and paper. Now we got us a book. Who can we sell it to?"

It seemed nothing about this business added up (super important since we want to make money) or made a lick of business sense. It reminded us of tossing Alice down the hole and watching her morph into Wonder Woman to sword fight the Queen of Hearts who gets in a good and unfair stab in the back … just to make one more gold coin. OK, we're digressing. We just don't want you to end up like Alice falling and tumbling into a black hole that is publishing today.

So the great publishing experiment began. We're not women who live and die by anyone's rules. If we did, our newsletters and books wouldn't be half as amusing or unique; and therefore, not as popular either. The very first question we had to ask, "Why is the publishing industry struggling?" We've heard the stories. We even had our printer tell us the stories of self-published authors with sheds full of their last books that didn't sell. We realized you had two different extremes butting up against each other. On one end, traditional publishers who pay small royalties, make it extremely difficult to get manuscripts in front of readers, and have very odd sales procedures like buybacks (ever heard of any consumer product being purchased back if it doesn't sell?); and on the other end, you have self publishing that involves publish on demand and some services that weren't paying off for the authors either. And what the author got in return could be described aptly as "crap" (there's that word again).

So without asking any questions about what is or is not broken per se, we began looking at other industries that made money and were not in decline. For example, we were already co-owners of the marketing and public relations firm called M Communications (www.mcommunicationsnc.com). Marketing and publishing agencies have a billable-hours system set up and retainers much like legal firms. Consumers of

> **Smart Girls:**
> Someday I hope to write a book where the royalties will pay for the copies I give away.
> ~ Clarence Darrow

services also called clients purchase services one at a time or spend money on a monthly fee or retainer to receive X number of services or hours. They then make monthly payments that enable the agency to count on a steady revenue stream. This system makes it more affordable for clients who can purchase a number of often expensive services and spread the cost out over many months much like a car payment.

So we wondered, well, why would this type of set up not work for publishing too? Self publishers often pay editors and designers for service — and then go out and get public relations professionals too. So it made sense that since we already did marketing and public relations and had the publishing background, why not set up a publishing "agency" and run it the same way? So we began setting up a menu of service based on standard metrics. Metrics measure time required to do X, Y, Z services, such as ghostwrite, edit a manuscript, design a cover, design the guts, and then do the marketing and public relations support, including websites, press releases and media kits.

Now to back up a minute, this really started because 2L's first book *Second Bloom* won several awards and authors started asking her to publish their books too. So, before 3L ever officially opened its doors, we had a line of authors in wait to make it official, which gets back to the answer to the question: How are we going to do this? We knew the basics — editorial, design and production. What we didn't know was how to really make this work from an operations standpoint. Yet through a lot of bumbling around (we bumbled and admit it), we literally stumbled onto solutions.

A Royal Flush

No, not as in flush my profits … we mean true-blue royalties that have a significant and meaningful ROI that you can, in fact, take to the bank. Come on let's get honest. We're in this to make money. No, we won't sugarcoat this fact. We all have to pay mortgages and eat — plain facts of life. It seemed to us that the current industry was set up to do one clear thing — keep the publishers fat and happy. How's that working for them? So, we needed to figure out how to maintain operations without charging our authors, who in most cases are individuals just like us trying to make a decent living.

We toyed with the cost per book. OK, we would charge a percentage of each book sold and the author would keep the rest. Yet we found that when we already charge for services this didn't seem to be palatable or fair to the authors. So, 2L got confused by what 1L said about the charge process and through a jumble of thinking came up with 18 percent surcharge *added to the print bill*. Now this made it much more manageable for the author and ultimately a minor amount charged per book. While smaller print runs only cover the cost of the ISBN numbers and the upload of the titles into the various distribution systems, it pays off in the end when a book goes nuclear and rises up the sales charts.

> *Smart Girls:*
> "The difference between genius and stupidity — genius has its limits."
> ~ Unknown

We wish we could brag ... oh yeah! We're sooo brilliant; but honestly what we just described is the intellectual process that led to so-called brilliance. I guess you could compare it to Einstein saying something like, "Oh, now *that* sounds *relatively* good." OK, now you know — smart by default. An interesting concept — and we are definitely laughing if you thought we sat down in a meeting and thought up the Hybrid Model. Umm, that is a big no.

Conquest of the Amazonian

Next up is the question: How do we distribute our books? Self-published books litter the Amazon highway, and so we knew that Amazon would be the avenue toward national distribution. Little did we know that Amazon is really a beast we'll call Ama-kong. Just so you know, we don't own ... or more importantly *control* Amazon (although we wish we did). We quickly discovered Ama-kong has a mind of its own. Want to talk to a human

> *Smart Girls:*
> "But why, why, why, why is my book listed as 'out of stock.' Can't you call them?"
> ~ Disgruntled author

being, because your book has been listed as *out of stock* for three weeks? Too bad. Want to fix a technical glitch on the site by talking to a human? Too bad. Want to know why Ama-kong put your book on sale without your permission and ask a human? Too bad. Upset because they put your book on sale. Too bad. Upset because it has been accidentally listed out of stock for three months running. Too bad. See … it's all just too bad for you — and that is how it goes … too bad.

The good news: We have our director of operations who knows every detail about how Amazon works. She does an excellent job of managing it. And how did we learn to pass the buck and not try it ourselves. We tried it! Yeah, get your hands dirty and realize you'll never have time to wash them so … here hire someone. And so it goes with Amazon. If our operations manager tells you some quirky rule about Amazon, don't bother to question it. She knows her stuff.

National Distribution – Easy Peezy

Next up, how were we going to do what traditional publishers do — get your book into the major retail chains? It was the last question to be answered in the process. If we didn't have distribution, we would be no different than other self publishers. Here is the real deal. We really didn't agonize too much over it. We discussed the question a couple of times; but one day magic happened. 2L was on the phone with a distribution house for a completely unrelated conversation. As she glanced over their website she realized they offered national distribution. A few questions later and a big, fat "yes" and 3L went national. We're not going to reveal anymore than the fact that we have it — and our authors have it too.

60 Percent Royalties – OMG! Really?

Yes, across all of major sales channel the royalty amounts vary, but when averaged out they come out to roughly 60 percent. Now some channels pay higher than others. Books sell differently through the various channels too. So to suggest that each author receives a flat 60 percent is misleading. If your book sells super well through Amazon, most of your sales will be at 45 percent; but let's compare … 45 percent to 15 percent from a publishing house. Still sounds better to us. We also do a number of major events per year and do table sales that our authors enjoy an 80 percent royalty from. It was 100 percent in the early days, but we soon found the overhead costs were killing us. When we switched up the authors didn't flinch. Again, 80 percent is unheard of. So who cares, right?

Also to emphasize a point we just made. Each book sells its own way. We cannot predict where the top sales will come from. Sometimes a book will sell really well off the table sales and not Amazon — that would be our book *Smash*. Other times, a book flies off Amazon and that would be *Fertile Kitchen*. It all just depends. We suspect *Fertile Kitchen* does well online, because fertility and reproduction are very intimate, family-oriented, and most importantly personal matters one does not want to broadcast. So, couples can order the book in the privacy of their own homes. Now will *Fertile Kitchen* sales continue to be bigger on Amazon than national purchases in bookstores? We won't know for a few more months, but nothing about the public's purchasing behavior is predictable. We try to teach our authors not to try and figure it out, but let the sales figures reveal buying patterns and leverage it.

A Single Umbrella Keeps Us All Dry

Next up, 3L Publishing doesn't send its authors out on a scavenger hunt to find publicity and marketing services. We don't leave our authors out in the frozen tundra to die from hypothermia when it comes to marketing their books, which honestly most authors don't have a clue. They can artistically write, but few writers have the combined business and creative heads.

We understand that authors aren't experts when it comes to marketing; and therefore, we added our marketing and PR chops to the contract to save more money from accidentally falling into an unscrupulous agency's pockets. No offense to our own professional cousins; but most marketing and PR account executives are clueless about how to manage authors' needs. They are typically used to dealing with big corporate giants that can afford to spend $5,000 a month on a retainer. We know that is crazy for a small author to even consider.

So what we've done is create integrated programs, which means authors can purchase both publishing and marketing services all from the same company. For less than it costs to purchase a standard retainer, authors receive a publishing and marketing campaign, including the necessary website. We don't leave guesswork for the author to figure out. And this figuring seems to involve the author having to ask around and hopefully stumble on the right resources, which can be hit or miss when they don't know what to look for or to expect.

Here's the nasty rub: Many authors get "taken" — and not in the romantic kind of way. No we're talking bamboozled. Bigger is not better. Just because you do fork over $5,000 for a month for a year doesn't mean you'll see results. You will largely be ignored in a sea of other clients who pay way more than you do — and like any hungry and expensive child that screams get the most attention.

Another advantage: 3L staff knows and understands your book by the time it's published. So when the marketing takes place, no misunderstanding exists. We will also clearly have firsthand statistics on sales trends to better strategize your campaign. So, once again the author wins — and you can clearly understand why 3L is thriving even when the industry is not.

The Down Low with Hybrid Publishing

Smart Girls:

When twelve-year-old Penny is handed a pad the "size of an ironing board cover," she cries out "Do I have to do this from now till I die?" The answer is, of course, no, at which point she replies, quite relieved, that there is something "to look forward to."

~ Marge Percy

The real deal about New Publishing: It's the wave of the future. The music industry has adopted a similar model. What New Publishing says, "Hey, author you are a partner in your success." It turns the publisher-author relationship into a symbiotic one where each relies on the other to succeed. It doesn't extricate and pull certain parts of the process apart. Everything you will ever need as an author is provided under the New Publishing umbrella. Do we sound biased? Yes! But we're both writers — and we developed this business from an author's point of view, which gave us a tremendous leg-up when it comes to getting it — that is, getting it *right*.

Chapter 8: Publish on Demand ... You didn't! Yes, you did ...

*"There ain't nothing that breaks up homes, country and nations like somebody **publishing** their memoirs." ~ Will Rogers*

Did they really just publish that? *Really?* When it comes to publish on demand (POD), no real rules of publishing "engagement" exist. You pay and they take your money. There is no quality control unless you wish to purchase additional services (at a cost, of course), and while some authors wish to delude themselves and call their POD their "publisher," we'll use that term loosely. We're not talking Penguin here. The manuscript did not go through a vetting process. In fact, it went through little or no process at all. You can purchase package services that will prep your book (or any old book you wish to publish), give you perhaps two cover design choices (or design your own), and do pre- and post-production work.

You tell them how many copies you want at a time and for a whopping $6 to $7 a copy you can have as many as you like. Just realize that if you sell your soft-cover book for $12.95, the average going rate, you will make very little money after you've paid for it. Do you get anything beyond copies delivered to your doorstep? No, you get what you pay for. Oh, well, they might put it on Amazon for you and take another huge slice out the usual 55 percent Amazon already takes.

We have seen more horror stories with POD companies than not. This is not to say all POD companies put out a bad product; we have seen one quality book out of several hundred over the last year. The larger POD companies are household names — i-Universe, Lulu, Lightspeed (which are also self publishing) — and countless others. Most of these companies' headquarters don't even reside on U.S. soil. So, many of the gross errors often occur because a Chinese English-speaking editor worked on your manuscript — that is, in English by the way.

So, it's not terribly surprising that the country that also put lead in children's toys also produces books with poor paper quality, which seems to be the norm in most POD books. By poor paper quality, we mean yellow … not white. Please do not get us started on some of the book covers we have seen. More often than not, the authors have zero input on the cover. Our personal favorite disaster is a memoir book for a grandmother with what appears to be a 22-year-old woman on the cover. Do you see how this does not make sense? We have also observed they will provide editorial services, which would be a plus except the books we have seen are loaded with spelling errors and other mistakes — the worst one being an actual page in a book with the heading: "The following items are missing from the table of contents." Unfortunately, we are not joking.

Smart Girls:

"Judge me all you want, but keep the verdict to yourself."
~ Unknown

If you are looking to use POD, we highly recommend you ask for references and samples of work before you invest your money or time. Again, not all of these companies produce poor work; however, you need to protect yourself and thoroughly research them before signing on. Typically, these books are also not best sellers because most companies do exactly what POD infers … publish on demand. You do get as many copies as you "demand" at $6-$7 apiece.

So, sure they'll print a limited run say of 500, but then guess what? You're on your own sister. You have to sell those copies yourself with absolutely no guidance. Now this works if you don't want to pay a large print bill upfront and you lack confidence that you'll generate high-volume sales, which in reality without marketing and PR help you will not — so no problem right — that is, if you think small. So, PODs are great if you want to write a book to hand out at seminars or small events; but if you intend to become a best-seller using a POD, good luck to you. Of course, we honestly don't want to discourage or dissuade folks who need a limited print run for a seminar from going this route either. It's just important that you know the pluses and minuses and identify what exactly is your goal.

Beware PODs Masquerading as Independent Publishers

An area of concern comes from small publishers that are really only a notch beyond self publishing but position themselves as a "major" publisher complete with the bongs and gongs (anything semi related to the gong you know has to be bad). Some small presses with names like "Hamster" Press (seriously, we want to know why publishers choose names related to wild animals or fur pelts ... where exactly is the connection? We seem to have missed it) or "Fake Fur" Publishing masquerading as independent publishers, but really use POD services to produce their final products. So the book comes out and looks no different than anything ordered from a POD service.

These independent publishers may or may not provide national distribution, but watch out here too. One author we know used a publisher we'll call Fake Fur Publishing out of a small town in the Midwest. "Fake Fur" Publishing used a distributor we'll call "Zing" that had this rather strange business practice. "Zing" would order some 500 copies from "Fake Fur" Publishing and two weeks later ship the copies back, which the author had to pay for anyway. The author became suspicious that some under-the-table shenanigans must have been going on between "Fake Fur" and "Zing" when it came to shipping costs and lining their pockets.

Just do your homework when you work with an independent press. Do they do their own work in-house and print with a regular printer or are they working with a POD? If they're working with a POD, which one are they contracted to do work with? You want to know what quality of work the POD produces since ultimately the book will, in fact, be produced by the POD. What are their distribution practices? Ask them outright if they play the shipping-back-to-you game. Just say, what happens if "Zing" ships the book back? Do I have to pay for those shipments? How frequently and how many books do they ship back? And if they talk out of two sides of their mouth, and you regularly write big checks for returns of 500 that were ordered and shipped back within the same week, something definitely smells stinky in Denmark. Don't be duped; terminate your contract no questions asked.

Batteries Not Included and Tons of Assembly Required

> **Smart Girls:**
>
> **Marissa:** "Someone was in my room."
> **Mason:** "Yeah mine too. I think we got elves."
> ~ Batteries Not Included (1987)

There are several items that are not included if you choose to do go the POD route so we are going to be pretty blunt (shocking) and let you know the bad before the good. Bad news numero uno: You will not get an advance with POD. This may seem pretty obvious if you know about traditional publishing and know how difficult it is to get an advance with that model; however, we need to point this out to those who are just starting their research within the publishing realm. Just remember that POD is a similar animal to self-publishing, because you are still predominantly doing it yourself with a little extra help.

> **Smart Girls:**
>
> The guy who runs the place is a little temperamental, especially about the ordering procedure. He's secretly referred to as the Soup Nazi."
> "Why? What happens if you don't order right?"
> "He yells and you don't get your soup."
> ~ Jerry and Elaine in "The Soup Nazi"

You additionally will not receive national distribution with the POD model. What does this mean? *No Borders and Barnes and Noble for you!* And if you're deluding yourself that you can apply and win national distribution on your own, we have more bad news. Most distributers do not distribute individual titles; but don't completely despair yet. Small independent publishers that may use POD may also have an agreement with a distributor like "Zing" or they may work with our distributor that uses multiple distribution channels, but 3L's distributor on average takes 38 percent of each book it sells. So, if your independent press uses POD at $7 a book, you pay for the printing of each book (which is usually the case if we failed to mention that as well) and sell it through 3L's distributor at 38 percent return, how much do you get back?

Let us put it in concrete details. One of our authors used a small press out of the Bay Area that utilizes a POD to print her book. Every six months she receives a check for $12 — we can't even feed a family of four at McDonald's for $12 anymore. Not good. And how much do you suppose that is per hour? (One little detail about our distributor: You must ship them a minimum of 550 books to distribute through them.)

Smart Girls:

Who needs national distribution anyway when I can sell my book at the elementary schools' annual book fair!

Now you can apply for individual distribution through major players such as Bakers and Taylor or Ingram by going through groups like the Independent Book Publishers Association; but guess what! They only accept 50 titles a year (out of thousands) and from what we could tell, the nature of the criteria wasn't particularly obvious. Your book could be the next prize winner — as 2L's book won five awards and got rejected — and still be turned away for any number of reasons, including the name on the spine is too small; the font is *different*; the cover doesn't pop; the chapters look strange; and what's that "thing" on the cover ... and so it goes — all of it is often superficial and subjective.

One thing we noticed on these rejections that we found rather frustrating — it appeared the committee didn't even read the book. So, how would they know one way or the other if it's good, bad, ugly or trash-worthy? Imagine your book rejected based a perfunctory cruise of your spine and cover. Oh, but hell! Who needs distribution anyway? Well, you do if you seriously intend to sell more than 50 copies to friends and family. First, you cannot do book signings in the big bookstores unless your book is in the "system" (meaning the distributor's database). The big stores — excluding the random local Borders — will not allow you to do book signings in the store without being able to order your books and stock their shelves.

So what's an author to do? Well, you can do signings at independent bookstores — and be subjected to endless negative talk by the bookstore owner who will puff up his chest and beat it with words of warning, death and plague about how terrible "it is out there" for authors. Puffed-up chest-beater will also tell you, "You'll never get on Oprah," and live to eat his words when Oprah's book club editor does call about your book. So, spare yourself the aggravation and chest beating and care about whether or not your book gets a distributor behind it.

We can promise you one thing for certain when it comes to using a POD and ensuring you have distribution. You can always get your book distributed through Amazon. Will your POD publisher manage this for you? The answer is sometimes (for a big chunk of your sales) — and we wish you the very best of luck here. The author of the previously mentioned Grandma book said her POD sent her a check from Amazon sales for a whopping $50 about once every six months. Well, lucky you. Now you can at least upgrade your Happy Meal to a bucket of KFC.

Would you like more negative news? Well, whether you would like to hear this or not we are going to elaborate further. We bet by now you are wondering about royalty payments. The answer here is there are none — royalty payments are only received when you publish with the New Publishing or traditional model. When you use POD, you pay for services — again, POD is an outgrowth of self publishing. Now you do keep 100 percent of each book you sell ... well, let us rephrase. You can keep 100 percent of the 50 percent that is gross profit. So, you pay $6 a book and sell it for $12 and you make $6 a book. If you sell thousands that sounds great, right? Well, let's continue our math exercise. Pay $6 x 1,000 = $6,000 in hard costs and you keep $6,000, but guess what else. Did you have to spend money on marketing (see below) to sell that 1,000? Did you build a website? How much did that cost? Can you see your "profits" eroding quickly?

How about this grim reality: You can make more writing for a national magazine a 2,000-word feature story at $2 a word. You catch the bottom-line effect? You make more money on an article versus a book — and which one took more work do you suppose?

It's POD – Is that contagious? Does it itch?

Oh come on! Give me some good news now please! Well … we dearly want to, but we're saving the best for last (no, not really). If you want to hire your POD publisher for marketing, you are out of luck too. Marketing will be discussed more in a later chapter but by marketing we mean: media kit, website, newsletter and more. We have to be honest because this is a case-by-case basis as to whether or not POD providers do a good job in this area.

So far, we cannot say we've seen anything remotely well done; but we can emphatically suggest we've seen some pretty scary media kits. By scary, we mean unprofessional and will undoubtedly make the media professionals roll their eyes and delete — and the collateral materials are overly branded with the POD company name. Who are they promoting? You or them? Anyway, this is just some food for thought. The POD model will also typically offer publicity services too — yaye! You need to have a publicist … period. We can tell you that the two author clients of ours who did not invest in publicity services have their books sitting and not selling. As for the type of publicity you will receive, this is something you need to ask about.

Again, we were hoping to share some great PR success stories (finally); but instead we have only witnessed disastrous POD PR programs such as one article per month over a six-month period with zero coverage, and this is at $3,000 per month. We have also seen zero coverage, minimal media contacted, but one interview with the publishing company's radio channel. Yet as we just mentioned you're facing a *Catch-22* anyway (wait … isn't that a book too). The reason your POD PR department cannot get good press is because the press knows it's a POD-produced book. So, they can't get the press' attention, but your book needs the press' attention to help it sell — and round we go.

If you are not mandated to sign up for a PR program, it doesn't matter. You absolutely must research the POD provider's PR services and most importantly ask about their results. If you fail to do your homework and check whether or not their clients received even a single headline or mention, then don't come to us crying in your Wheaties about how you got ripped off and now cannot afford a real publicist.

Oh hey! We have a better idea ... just screw the marketing anyway. Did we mention that the media will most likely not cover POD-type books? Yes, they know the big POD names — and since the POD publishers keep their logo squarely branded on your book and press releases (when they sell that service) the media knows the real scoop — and it's not a good one. What they know that most POD neophytes don't? That POD produces crap (there goes that word again) — and busy editors and producers have little time for the good stuff let alone the crap. So, your book loses credibility no matter how good or how bad and gets largely ignored by the media, which doesn't bode well for your sales. Isn't this like chasing your own "tale?"

Why Yes, Sally, We do Have Something Good to Say

> *Smart Girls:*
> "All over the flip of a goddamn coin."
> ~ Rules of Engagement (2000)

We now will focus on some of the positive aspects of the POD mode. With POD, you do not need to pay an agent a commission, but you do need to pay your print bill on individual print runs. Again, the benefit is you decide how many copies you want to have — and to further explain this benefit we are talking about 50 copies versus 1,500 copies. The author will still pay for all services under this publishing model, but the main positive here is that you really do save on your print bill; however, if you really want to save a lot of money, this model is ineffective for print runs larger than 1,000 — and very few traditional print houses will take smaller book print runs under 1,000.

So, at $6 a copy at $50 copies that makes sense. At $6 a copy for 1,000 copies that makes no sense since you could have it done on a larger print run with a traditional printer where you pay $1.50 a copy. Do the math and you can see the significant difference: $6,000 or $1,500 — it seems fairly obvious when you add it up. And the economies of scale continue to go down as the print run grows larger say upward of 5,000 copies where you can get your book down to .80 cent a copy — big, big difference girlfriends.

The main positives for using a POD are as follows: the author retains copyright, approves and agrees with editorial revisions, and will have a finished product within three to six months. The author will also not have to buy back their book from overstock in the event the book is not selling like the traditional model. This is a big positive but the reality is the POD models really only want you to sell 100 copies so they really do not care. Can we be any blunter? The answer here is "yes," but we want you to retain information versus revel in our mouthing off.

The main point we are trying to make with any model is to simply ask questions. As an author you need to ask about everything from cost to timeframe, and always keep in mind the return on investment. We are assuming you do not work for free or want to lose money in the process. The questions here are the key — and we hope you find the basic points helpful.

Chapter 9: Agents: Get out of their Pockets ... It Stinks Back Here

"This guy, with no office, no assistant, answering his own fuckin' phone, is willing to hip pocket me. Do you believe that shit?"
~ *Johnny Drama, Entourage*

OK, everything you've heard about agents is 100-percent true. Not kidding. They are often fast-talking, slick and slimy sales people. We do know one local literary agent that was soft spoken and genuinely nice; so don't count her in on that list of traits, but she is the exception *not* the rule. Can you tell this isn't going to be love-fest dedicated to all the agents we've known or will know? Yep, hard to give sincere praise to an industry designed to put a layer between artists and producers (publishers) and charges 15 percent for that added layer. To make matters worse, we have yet to work with a single agent we thought earned their keep, which makes it even more difficult to heap praise on the industry.

Now not to bash all agents — and we will say literary agents are a nicer breed than most — but in our experience we've never met a single agent we felt worth the investment. Problem is, if you intend to go the traditional publishing route you have no choice but to get an agent; it's how they play the game with traditional publishing; and it's also yet another reason why we're not fans. Now we understand the need to vet the quality of the work before it gets sent and clogs an already-full pipeline — but the blatantly exclusionary nature of the industry makes it frustrating for most artists.

First, we can speak to literary agents that represent both books and screenplays. A primary problem in Hollywood in particular is that they tend to qualify the process through the "I-know-someone" club not necessarily through talent.

Smart Girls:

Agent: I'm having a great day!
Writer: That's nice, how so?
Agent: My t-cell count is up.
Writer: Um, ah, are you sick?
Agent: Yes, I'm dying.

So unless you have a valid connection to an agent from someone willing to vouch for your ability to not just write, but write something good (as discerned by this potentially untrained friend) then you probably won't get an agent's attention. And if you're not in the "club," and you do manage to get an agent to review your book chances are the agent is new to the business, not very well connected, and desperately seeks his or her first real client. Now if you don't mind starting out holding each other's hand through the process, this isn't necessarily a bad deal; but if you're already working full time somewhere and trying to get your first book or screenplay sold, well, it's no cherry on the sundae. Because ...

Most agents aren't hungry enough to do what they're paid to do. We know this is going to offend agents; but Michelle (2L) had two different agents — and in both cases, she had to do the dirty work. What does that mean exactly? It meant a lot of phone calls to publishers or producers only after the agent mailed the "now-solicited" script (we'll get into the solicited and unsolicited), and then began the follow up, which while it seemed like the agent should perform such tasks were not happening.

Now an eager writer hopeful and wanting to break into the business will just go ahead, not argue, and do what needs to be done, which can involve dozens upon dozens of phone calls just to get the book read by the first layer of readers who give it "coverage" (a word you should become familiar with). The coverage then gets passed up to the acquisitions manager who reviews it, and so it goes. So while this takes place, you, the writer continue to pester and call and follow up to ensure it doesn't slip through the cracks.

The Notorious Hip-Pocket Situation

A "hip-pocket" situation happens most often to newbie writers who have little or no track record to encourage their agents to put their full attention on them.

Bigger, more well-known — and most importantly — well-connected agents tend to put low-level writers *into their hip pockets*, which means they will put out the book idea if (and that is a big *if*) a situation arises that might be a perfect opportunity. "Ah, I have something right here in my pocket …" get it?

It also means that book idea sits in the hip pocket where it goes through the wash to come out all mangled. A writer who has been "hip pocketed" will not enjoy the "perks" of the agent who actively sells his or her book. The agent is too big to care. They already have J.K. Rowling as their primary client or John Grisham. You're just a fascinating little want-to-be who maybe had a friend who begged them to take you or — an ex-wife who they owe a favor. 2L had an agent at the giant agency CAA for about a year. Yeah, she gave up her 10 percent all right. He did absolutely nothing but put his name on the contract. Can we spell the word s-u-c-k?

The real cautionary tale: Don't assume that because you got the likes of a guy or gal from CAA to represent your work it means anything either. It won't necessarily get your book sold. Why? Because the agent has to care enough to at least mention your manuscript to the proper contacts. If they're making $10 million a book off J.K. Rowling, why would they give a flying monkey about some unknown author that might bring in some chump change of say $5,000 — that is nothing more than a trip to the nearest Nobu restaurant for them. It may not even be enough to buy a high-class Swiss candy bar. Hence your book gets the "little" book treatment.

On the flipside, smaller agents can do the exact same thing. They might have more incentive to sell your book than the big guy, but it

> ### Smart Girls:
>
> **Adam Davies:** You should be a nicer person. Maybe then people wouldn't fuck you.
> **Ari Gold:** You talked, Davies?
> [Davies turns to leave]
> **Ari Gold:** Hey, Adam.
> **Adam Davies:** Yeah, Ari?
> **Ari Gold:** Just so you know, your girlfriend, when she was in the mailroom, offered to blow me. True story.
> ~ Entourage

doesn't take much in terms of sales to distract them away from you. They may have five mid-selling authors already, and your new-kid-in-town experience won't be anything more than clever and cute to them. They're too busy making sure they can pay their mansion mortgage payments with their mid-level guys or girls to really have time to play with the cute new puppy. And you know cute wears thin when the puppy isn't getting any interest and wets on the carpet. So why waste their time?

Solicitation — Not the Hooker Kind

The primary reason to get an agent — most publishers will not even look at what is called "unsolicited" manuscripts. A solicited manuscript must come from a reputable and accredited agent. You can't really blame New York or Hollywood for establishing these rules. Back in the "unsolicited" days, the publishing houses and studios wound up with nasty copyright infringement lawsuits on their hands and thousands of unreadable manuscripts. Now since 2L personally experienced what it's like to have an idea stolen, copyright infringement runs rampant. An unsolicited script without the appropriate papers signed for protection can lead to copyright infringement lawsuits, which the publishers don't want.

In order to install some protection, publishers began working only with accredited agency professionals and having the authors sign disclaimers that said they would not sue should a book come out too similar to the author's manuscript. A signed disclaimer can still be used in lieu of an agency agreement by independent authors, but the industry prefers to work with people it feels it can trust; hence, the well-established agency or agent. It affords a layer of protection.

On the flipside, authors should take great pains to protect their work too. You should at the very least include a copyright symbol © and date that suggests the intent to copyright and the date of publication. An author's recourse without official copyright is to prove he or she wrote the original material. The author would then have to produce a record of dates, meetings and times that track the history of the manuscript to prove it's their original work and not the suspected infringer's work. We don't know about you — but can you say

P.I.T.A. (Pain in the Ass)? No thanks! So, make sure you protect yourself from copyright infringement by registering it with the U.S. Copyright Office (www.copyright.gov). Or do the poor girl's copyright and send a sealed copy of your manuscript to yourself with the post date stamped on it.

The Ultimate Catch-22 in Literature

The difficult problem in this situation means that publishers will not look at unsolicited material. You can call and call to your heart's content, but you will hear the same answer over and over again: *We do not accept unsolicited manuscripts.* Some of the smaller, independent publishing houses will accept them; but the big publishers in New York generally do not. And here lies the ultimate Catch-22. You can't get an agent without a book published, and you can't publish a book without an agent. And here you go spinning in circles — and feeling frustration created from this exclusive literary club that is very difficult to join.

This exclusionary club mentality drives us completely bonkers. What you now have in is an elitist mentality that requires authors to have the "right" friends to get published. The merits of the work have been officially flushed away to be replaced with the "old friend's" club. Just because you happen to be friends with someone as famous as Stephenie Meyer, author of the *Twilight* series, doesn't mean you know how to write anything. Yet this "friendship" can be parlayed into an introduction to a world-famous agent (Stephenie's agent), who probably owes her fortune to Stephenie and is not about to say no. Stephenie's agent out of obligation takes on the project and there you go. Mediocrity peddled to New York where some editor also owes Stephenie's agent a favor. Ever wondered how some bad books get published? We just told you. Of course, if you're Stephenie's friend you're really happy and who cares how it got published.

Ari-etta Gold Super Agent

Now we don't want to make generalizations. You have exceptions to every rule, and some genuine talent can break through these barriers just fine. You may even be the one author who disagrees with everything we've just written based on an exceptional experience with your agent. We're happy you're happy. It's quite possible that you can have a genuine and sincere partnership with your agent — and perhaps be friends. An agent who gets behind your project is absolutely priceless. This person — if they're a super whiz-bang powerhouse — might even procure an advance for you. Wouldn't that be cool?

We do honestly believe that tenacity, perseverance and passion will break through all barriers; but we also want you to understand the barriers do exist. Author-agent love affairs are not the rule, they are the exception. Once you're aware of the challenges then you can indeed shrug them off, but just don't get trapped by them. Ending up as a hip-pocket client won't feel good should you be the recipient. Heck we didn't even know the expression "hip pocket" existed until it happened to us; but as you can see, we didn't let it stop us from doing what we're doing now.

We just want writers to know how the business works. You don't need an agent to work with 3L … thank goodness. If you did, we wouldn't be able to write honestly about agents lest we get black listed; but since we have no vested stake in the agent industry, we can share what we've experienced first-hand and give you information important to your success.

Chapter 10: Queries, Synopsis ... the Necessary Evils

"'Classic.' A book which people praise and don't read."
~ Mark Twain

Why does mere mention of a synopsis or book proposal send writers into hyper drive to avoid it? Writers will pull their hair out, scream, and throw a fit before they'll force themselves to sit down and start writing something about what they've just written. The "adult" tantrum can go on for weeks, months and even years — and to the author's detriment prevents their book from getting sold. Many authors would rather have their fingernails yanked out than be forced to write those miserable things called a query or synopsis. Yet traditional publishers and 3L will not even glance the author's way without one.

Smart Girls:

"Never write a letter while you are angry."
~ Chinese Proverb

"Write when you're pissed, read it to your business partner, and delete the email. Then change their name and make fun of them in your future newsletter and on your radio show."
~ 3L Publishing

Let us be very, very clear. You *need* to write a query letter or synopsis — and you need to do not just a good job but an excellent one. A busy publisher will not even glance at your book without first reading the cover letter or proposal. They have zero time to read your entire book — so don't delude yourself that *your* book is so riveting and fantastic that they would make *you* the exception. Just take your Xanax Francesca, and keep praying and drinking. You need to write a query letter and synopsis in order for publishers to even consider looking at your full manuscript. This is most important in the case of a work of fiction. We receive new proposals every day — and if we get through page 10 of a manuscript you are very, very lucky. If you get a response, even if it is not positive be polite and continue to submit elsewhere.

Enquiring Minds Want to Know

Let's now assume you are a professional writer — and if you are a true professional you're steps ahead of the rest and can probably draft a well-written query letter; however, if you're a math teacher by day who has somehow managed to write a novel by night, then we recommend you procure professional editing services to help draft your letter. Your query letter is the single most important document you are going to write, because it may be the only intro to your work a prospective publisher will read. And we have absolutely one guarantee for those who recklessly submit queries full of grammar mistakes and typos. Your letter will go no further than the nearest "special file" — and your book will sadly never be read.

Most publishing houses are inundated with new manuscripts daily, and publishers like reading these letters because they are short. If you think that your manuscript is "da-bomb," and you can skip this process and submit the whole thing; you are dead wrong my friend. Now, when we say by *letter,* we don't mean handwritten with a stamp. Email works just as well — and it is preferred in most cases. Plus, you will be helping to save the rainforest.

Your query letter should be short and to the point and address your audience. By audience do not say that your book will appeal to the mass American population of the United States unless you are a former president. Please be specific — otherwise publishers will think you are full of something that rhymes with "it." If you read this right now and wonder who your market is and if your book is marketable, please close this book and smack yourself on the side of the head with it ... again. OK, did any sense just ring through? If yes, continue ...

You should have researched the marketability of your topic *prior* to writing it, Lenny. Oh and "hello," your audience is the group that will purchase your precious novel. No audience = no points = no money to pay the light bill. And just to add to the conundrum that is publishing: Do you know how many books sit gathering dust on the shelf that someone did, in fact, analyze the market — and it didn't matter? It's a tough, tough book-buying market public friends. So, do everyone a favor and at least try even if the sales results don't happen the way the survey says.

We bet about now you wonder how long your letter should be? If you are sending this via U.S. Postal Service, please keep it to a page — and if you are doing the email thing, please keep it to a couple of paragraphs. To reiterate, do not send an entire novel about your novel — please keep it brief and interesting. And please place your hand on this good book and swear you will not under any circumstances send what is essentially a book-length letter, because you just couldn't leave *anything* out. Your reader will receive your 50-page query, roll her eyes, laugh to her sister reader, and say something like, "Hey 2L! Want to see this dumbass *letter?*" "Sure 1L." 2L will lug it up in the air, both women will giggle, and then 1L will gamely toss it in the trash as if she's scored a point in basketball. OK, that scene doesn't bode well for your future.

Please keep your letter professional too. Quadruple check for spelling, punctuation and grammar errors — this may be your only shot. Also, *do not write how you talk.* For example:

> "Dear ABC Publishing House:
> OMG, I am like so totally excited about my book because it is totally like the best piece of work you will EVER read. My main character, Martha tells her Dad that she should like get a red Mustang for her 16th birthday, and he like gives her a bus pass instead. WTF is that all about? Totally UNCOOL. Anyway … I think it would be like the best book ever — and it be soooo awesome to get an advance too! I was thinking maybe like $1 million or you know whatever you think too. OMG, so excited!! Can't wait — oh, and you can text me too. I want to show all my girlfriends like the good news on my way-cool iPhone! ☺
> Cuddles!!!
> Jenni – Bear"

Please hire an editor if your letter looks anything like the above or if your manuscript looks like the above letter — don't bother. Just go back to bed and cuddle your "bear."

Last, please make sure that your letter has a hook — and we are not talking Captain Hook. You need to be able to explain in a very interesting way why your book should be published, and do not put the publisher to sleep with the first couple of sentences. No one wants to read a snooze-fest.

Synopsis — Not "Snot-Fest"

Another important piece of necessary evil involves the synopsis, and yes — you will need this too. A synopsis is difficult for many people to write because they try to sell their books. Most authors are not sales personnel and vice versa. Below are a couple of key points to writing a good synopsis — and we are going to start with a list of what to do.

> **Smart Girls:**
> **Rumack:** "Elaine, you're a member of this crew. Can you face some unpleasant facts?"
> **Elaine:** "No."
> ~Airplane

A synopsis is an outline of your novel in present-tense form. Some publishers only want two pages and some want 20 pages. If you cannot find out a specified length, we recommend sticking to 10 to 15 pages. Your publisher will want to know two things:

- Will the topics/character hold the interest until the very end of the story?
- Does the topic fit with the genre of what the publisher typically produces?

Now, before you submit your story, please do a little homework. If you submit a book of sonnets to a company that does not publish poems, you wasted everyone's time. Also, if you decide to not do your homework ahead of time, submit anyway, and then email a nasty response when the publisher responds with a pass, consider yourself forever doomed with said publisher; consider yourself an ongoing topic of bad submissions for said publishers radio show and newsletter; and last and worst of all — you will be blacklisted all because you acted like a complete ass.

Now we will get back to the list of what you need. Please see below for what you need for a synopsis:

- Please be sure to succinctly tell what the story is about; who the main characters are; and what their conflicts/goals are.
- Talk about the conflict in depth. Most novels involve a conflict that resolves itself by the end of the book. Please make sure this is interesting and not: "Ben lost his house keys and decided to take the day off work."
- Write your synopsis in the present tense and hook your reader with the setting, tone, style and pace.
- Do not be lazy and reproduce the first 10 pages of your novel and include all gripping dilemmas.
- Be sure to include all subplots that affect the main characters.

We hope this helps you create your synopsis ... while it may be painful for a writer to share everything when an editor has not requested to see your full manuscript; the point is to sell your manuscript so let your hair down. Be sure to follow any rules set by submission guidelines — if the rules say 10 pages don't be a pompous fart and assume your work is so good they will take time out to read 50 pages. Last, if you receive a request for a full manuscript, mark the email or package with "response" to your request or something of that nature. Your mail/email will otherwise get buried.

Smart Girls:

Margaret: "What am I allergic to?"
Andrew Paxton: "Pine nuts, and the full spectrum of human emotion."
~The Proposal

The book proposal ... otherwise known as the greatest brain damage bestowed upon humankind

Here is the deal: You sign with a company that offers national distribution you do not have to submit a book proposal and apply. The most painful thing about this is the fact that most distributors do not take individual titles so your efforts will be worthless, but you still have to jump through the hoops.

The book proposal whether requested after receiving a query letter from a publisher or whether you are applying for distribution includes the following elements and includes the synopsis as well. You will need to submit:
- Table of contents
- Sample chapters
- Synopsis
- Marketing Plan (and, ha, ha … if you have never written one of these before; pull out Kleenex box and buy *SMASH: A Smart Girls Guide to Practical Marketing and PR* while you are at it — you will need it).
- Reviews — think *NY Times* not Grandma Linda's Book Circle.

We hope you have enough information now to realize the necessary evils required … and yes, they certainly are.

Most book proposals go to independent distributors if you're a self-publisher. And as we mentioned earlier, most distributors make their determinations often based on no real evident guidelines. 2L's book *Second Bloom* won five publishing awards — and that impressive list of awards made absolutely zero impression on the distributors. It wasn't until 2L had a list of titles available from her publishing house that she was finally able to attain distribution. So, single titles and self publishing are tough turf — so write your proposal with your heart and passion on your sleeve and go for it. You may end up one of the handful that gains acceptance. And one more note: Some traditional publishers may first accept your synopsis and then ask for the proposal, and then finally ask for the book. It's not easy girlfriends, but a best seller will certainly make it worth the investment in the Rolaids.

Chapter 11: Really?! If You Happen to get a Call-Back New Rules to Not act like an A$$

"Stress: The confusion created when one's mind overrides the body's basic desire to choke the living daylights out of some jerk who desperately deserves it."
~ Author unknown

We don't know what it is about some writers — artistic temperament, immaturity, a need to blow off steam due to relentless rejection, Mommy took away my laptop when I was 12 … we don't know. What we do know is that when a 3L representative contacts some writers instead of doing the appropriate happy dance — a publisher is interested in my work — they take the stance of a cobra ready to strike and spit venom. No clue what that is about; but let's get real for a second. When you have been in search of a publisher, made perhaps dozens of queries, and submitted hundreds of sample chapters or queries — and you finally get the call you've been waiting for, turning into a territorial dog, seething, showing teeth, and ferociously barking will get you nowhere. So, let's discuss bad writer behavior you want to avoid — most especially with your prospective publisher.

Submit Not Omit

Some standard protocol exists when it comes to submitting your work. You should always start with a query and sample chapter (non-fiction), and a query, synopsis and sample chapter (fiction). A query and a sample chapter answer two important questions: What is this book about and how good

> **Smart Girls:**
>
> If you ever expect to get published, don't ever write this to a publisher: "You pass on me! Well, I pass on you!"

is the writing? As we noted earlier, if chapter one in your mind is your weakest chapter, please don't submit it. Weak is as weak does, meaning it will be an immediate strike against you, which we assume you don't want. You might also spend some money to have the sample proofed or at least edited. A sample chapter full of typos could be compared to anything full of typos. Does it send a message that you're a seasoned professional — or does it say, "I'm an amateur?" Which message do you want to send?

When In Doubt Spit It Out ... Or Don't Send It At All

Chapter one should be your best foot forward. It shows you understand book and storytelling structure. It shows off your writing and ability to establish the idea or story behind your book. It shows you have talent — or no talent at all. So, if chapter one somehow eludes you, and you lack confidence in it, but feel really good about the book, then get some help before you submit it. Go see a writing coach or ask a professional to make suggestions for improvement. Because here is the real deal. Once you have submitted a weak chapter one as a sample of your writing and skills — and it s-u-c-k-s, the publisher is done with you. They don't have time to coach or train you. You won't hear anything, or if you do it will be a rejection letter.

If your work is a piece of fiction, we're going to give you some very, very important advice. Do not submit the whole book, and in your tone and manner insist the publisher read the whole thing. When we ask for a synopsis, and the writer gets agitated and irritated with us — well, we end the conversation right there. We've actually had authors insist we read the whole book regardless. Some authors need to pick up 1L's famous clue phone. Do you understand what you're essentially "demanding" we do? You are "demanding" we spend up to two or three days of our valuable time reading your entire perhaps 400-

page manuscript — and to put the real acid in the heartburn, some authors then throw a tantrum when we explain that we don't have time.

Smart Girls:

"Miss Gwendolyn De Vere De Witt
Is having such a sulky fit!
Because she couldn't have her way
With other children at their play.
A sulky Goop I really call
As bad as those who cry and bawl."
~ Don't Be a Goop

Here is truth in advertising right from 3L and most publishers. We all need to get paid. Our time is money, and money pays the bills. In order for us to sit and read your entire book cover to cover, it would take hours if not days. Every hour spent for us at 3L is billable time. When we can't bill an hour to a paid project, we don't get paid — and we can't pay our bills. So why should we have to explain this at all? Like we just said, tantrum throwing often erupts when we tell authors to give us a sample and synopsis. The sample tells us if you can write. The synopsis tells us if the story is any good — or marketable … very simple. As noted earlier, we can tell literally by page one of a sample whether or not talent exists. Once we've determine talent and marketability, you're 10 steps ahead of the crowd.

Now when we sign a new author, of course, we read the whole book. In fact, we will have our nose deeply stuck in your book — and we will have nearly every chapter, character, foil and folly memorized. In some cases, we will have heavily edited those chapters and in other cases, we will have guided the writer through analysis and suggestion the story from adequate to stellar. Most authors who use our literary guidance end up thrilled beyond words to have that level of expertise involved in their projects. Most of these authors — by this time — understand the expertise and value of working with true professionals. And these authors typically won't make the next error we're about to describe.

The Argument Heard Round the Publishing World

What is next on our list of bad writer behavior? That would be the infamous argument with the editor that kills your book deal. We understand it's your book, and you've perhaps sweated many drops of blood into it. We get it; but we also have a proven track record as evidenced by all the 3L books gracing many retail shelves not just here in the states but around the world. So we definitely know what we're doing. When authors not just marry but obsess like a possessive spouse over their work, it becomes a point of discord and contention on the level of a civil war. We don't really like arguing much less arguing with a prospective author that we have not even signed yet.

If you're lucky enough to get a call from us, rule of thumb: Prepare yourself to listen and avoid arguing. We can't tell you just how many times an author gets a call and rather than do the formerly referenced happy dance, she instead decides to engage in a class debate about her book. Or worse when we're offering valuable insight about the market or marketing in general, decide we "don't know Jack" and take sides. Now assuming you don't have publishing, marketing or PR experience perhaps arguing with the experts might not be a very good start to a business relationship. In fact, you may find that you will never hear from 3L again.

One time, we had an author who wanted to publish a young Catholic cookbook call to discuss her book. After assuring us that all her friends loved the idea, she assumed we would jump right on board and publish it. Well, let's see here. Young Catholic market … niche. Young Catholic cooks … niche. Niche market = small potential = non-money maker. Hm … not good friends. So when we suggested she consider surveying the "young Catholic" market to find out interest in such a book, and she argued about it … hmm! What do you suppose happened to her — and her book idea? Yep, it went in the famous "special file."

The Will of Your Peeps … A.K.A., Peanut Gallery Opinions

Next up on the growing list of bad behavior involves what we'll call "inflicting the will of your peeps" on us. This is arguing part II — all based on your friend the high school English teacher who lives in Great Falls, Idaho who also loves your book, and why don't we? While most of you reading this must feel this sounds absurd, we sure wish everyone did and wouldn't use their friends, family and English teachers to determine that their manuscript is the next big best seller. First, while we won't say right to your face how silly this sounds, we are definitely emailing each other back and forth laughing. Come on! Your English teacher, really? Let's start with some basics when you use your friends and family as your critic's corner. They love you! They aren't going "diss" your manuscript. So, using your inner circle or "peanut gallery" as proof that your book is bound for the *New York Times* list, please don't — and please don't use it to somehow justify your point.

What you need to know ... even we don't know for sure what is going to be a best seller or what is not. All we can do is evaluate it based on our experience in the marketplace, and the merits of the writing and topic. Each book will take on its own selling patterns — and it can be challenging to figure that out. If it were easy, we would all be rich living in our seaside villas with the sound of waves crashing as our nightly lullabies; but since we're not that smart we can only use said experience — and really guess. Our guesses have turned out pretty accurate. Two books we surmised would be 3L top sellers have, in fact, proven us right. So, our instincts seem to be good ones, but you never know. 2L's first book *Second Bloom* had every indication it should be a top seller — it won five publishing awards after all. It was definitely the critic's darling yet it hasn't sold out its initial print run and made any meaningful money; on the flipside our book *Smash* paid itself off in two launch parties. So, one never knows.

Yet still even after we honestly tell some authors this information, they still bring up the peeps' opinions as a basis to persuade us they have the next *Harry Potter* on their hands. Oh, and they will talk in circles about how Aunt Zelda wrote a book in the '60s that sold 5,000 copies — and Aunt Zelda is convinced, absolutely convinced that your book on Hurricane Katrina will be a best seller. First, as we've already stated, we see zero marketability to be "milked" out of Hurricane Katrina —

Smart Girls:

Bubba: Have you ever been on a real shrimp boat?
Forrest Gump: No, but I've been on a real big boat.
~ Forest Gump

those books have come and gone. So unless it's really a book where Hurricane Katrina kind of shows up as part of the story (think *Forest Gump* and Hurricane Carmen's entrance to make him a rich shrimper) then we're going to take a "pass" — and we don't give a flying monkey what Aunt Zelda said. In fact, we find it borderline offensive that you honestly believe that Aunt Zelda knows more than a publisher. Again, not a good start to the business relationship.

"Well, Have You Ever Written a Best Seller?"

Next up is snotty behavior from already-published authors who feel compelled to shove their credentials down our throats. First, maybe not all publishers are as well-grounded as we are at 3L. We've already noted that traditional publishers have created quite a closed community. And we also understand rude behavior exists on both sides of the fence; but should you have an interest in publishing your next book with 3L and play the "Mrs. Snotty Pants" game with us, just go away. Your overly impressed view of yourself is nothing but annoying.

We've seen all levels of Mrs. Snotty Pants' behavior. From the author who once said right to our faces (why do it behind our backs, right), "You know a *real* publishing company ... no offense." I would have to point to the many 3L books to counter that statement. I guess ... because those books aren't *real*. Then you have the author who asks whether or not you would be interested in working out a publishing deal with some of her associates only to counter your sales pitch with, "Well, how many books have *you* sold? I wrote a best seller!" Or another author who was so threatened by us in some strange way, she at first said she consulted on our book (um not quite) and then brushed off the book as, "that red and black something or another."

You will also find a species of Mr. Snotty Pants who believes that name dropping will earn him some sort of odd respect from the "goo-gawkers" impressed that he knows such and such. First, name dropping isn't impressive. It tells us only one thing: you know such and such. Whoopee! A $1 and that name will get you a small cup of McDonald's coffee. Second, Mr. Name that Celebrity with a snotty lilt of thrill in his voice, only shows off some deep insecurity and need to prove he's *someone* because he knows someone he thinks is impressive and important — or needs to be fawned over by the "goo-gawkers." Whenever we end up around Mr. Name that Celebrity, we usually blankly nod. Name dropping isn't the name of the game ... that is, unless you need to impress upon an author you have the book club editor's name at Oprah to help them promote their book. Otherwise, who cares! We could drop A LOT of names with the rest of them, but we find that b-o-r-i-n-g and unnecessary. Who wants "goo-gawker" attention? It's just so ... *gooey*.

And our recent favorite comes from an author — not a publisher — who began to lecture us on publishing. How endearing was that experience? You know because he's such a *hot* author and all. He must know more about our business then we do. Oh, and then he passes me his business card and suggests maybe we should publish his next book. *Really?*

We Know You're Not a Goop!

We are describing behavior that falls into the minority. The only reason we're taking a whole chapter on it is mostly to entertain you; but for those "goops" out there who have perpetrated any of the described errors, please stop. You're not helping or advancing your careers. When 3L calls, do the happy dance, really! You should feel thrilled to be pulled out of literally hundreds of submissions and tagged as an author of interest. We wouldn't be calling if we didn't see potential; but cutting an immediate attitude based on whatever issue you have won't help get you published. Be open, respectful and listen.

And just because we don't immediately throw our credentials around, realize that 3L wouldn't exist at all if there wasn't substance behind the name. We don't feel the need to describe our abundant experience to you, read our website bios, and do some homework before you start trying to impress upon us why you know more than we do. And if you occasion to see the stack of rejected manuscripts on our desks, you would so get it! Your book *is* special, or we wouldn't have taken the discussion to the next level. So ... please! Happy dance!!

Chapter 12: Finally! My Baby! Now What? Marketing Time!

"I had a mother lined up for him, but she's bangin' the Pepperidge Farm guy and the kid won't stop peeing and throwing up, he's like a cocker spaniel."
~ *Big Daddy*

Want to know the number #1 mistake authors make? Their book is published. They're holding it proudly in their hands. They don't have any marketing prepared to support its release; they have no plans for a public relations campaign (see next chapter); and they don't have a budget for marketing. They call us some three weeks later and complain they have only sold books to family and friends. Why is their Amazon ranking so high (high is bad)? Why aren't they selling books? Our pat answer, "No one knows your book exists so why would they know to buy it?"

Book marketing takes time, money, resources, passion and commitment. You cannot publish a book — whether through self-publishing, traditional or New Publishing — and expect to sit back in your home and sell millions. This would be akin to sitting in your house and expecting monkeys to swing past your window — and I'm pretty sure that unless you live in Africa that *probably* isn't going to happen. If we can tell you anything meaningful in this book, you have to realize you will play an active role in the marketing process. No house sitting. No monkey watching. No hoping. No wishing.

You will need some essential tools that we'll get to in a moment, and you will have to pound the pavement, shake some hands, do book signings, perform at some speaking engagements, and sell this book. Those writers who cry, "shy," and, "I'm not outgoing," will find their books languish on the shelf and gather inches of unsightly dust. You have to be the face of your book. You will be delighted to find out how many people will purchase a book just because the author is present to sign a copy; however, not present and no deal. When we sell books at the various events we attend around the country, nothing sells a book faster than an excited, engaged and enthusiastic author.

And just know that acting the opposite — sitting and folding your arms behind the counter kills sales just as fast. It sends a negative message — especially if you have a self-help book about living your life in positivity, and you look downright hostile and pissed off. She glances at her watch and mutters, "When's lunch … this is so boring?" She groans just as a client sees the dower look on her face and runs for fear of being yelled at, "Hey! You're touching the books! Don't touch the books with *your* greasy fingers."

Book Marketing Basics … Or "Ah, Man! Do I really need a website?"

Authors love the writing process; but mention marketing and their enthusiasm wanes and their expressions shift into big sad faces. Most writers have great talent and artistic skills, but the business head often doesn't come with the same left-brain and right-brain abilities — and for gosh sakes please don't mention accounting to a writer. They will wince, throw a rock at you, and run for the hills. Accounting! Ew! Yet marketing and accounting matters to any business — and believe us when we say that your book is your business and needs to be treated that way. Authors who fail to recognize this fact often get duped, hustled and ripped off. Don't be roadkill smashed on the side of the publishing highway that everyone looks away from — gross! What a mess.

This means you must seriously approach your book and its very-necessary marketing — and if you suck at marketing then realize you should not attempt to do it yourself. Put down that pre-made website template, quit pushing those fonts around in Word, and get real. Why would you hire an amateur marketing person (you) and put your most precious "baby" in an amateur's hands. 3L Publishing deliberately includes marketing and PR in its menu of services. We found so many authors floundering when it came to the sales and marketing side — especially those folks who attempt to do it on their own.

The Marketing Square Dance — No Ruffled Petticoats, Please

When it comes to marketing books — or a business for that matter — you should include four fundamental tools in your marketing toolbox. These tools are geared toward leveraging viral marketing and will also support your public relations activities, which we will explain more in chapter 12. These tools are as follows.

Website – You absolutely must have a website. An author website should include about the book, author bio, seminar information if the author is planning to do that, news and updates, and purchase information. Most authors' websites don't need to be any larger than four pages — and it should be professionally written and designed. It should match the brand look and feel of your book, which of course, has been professionally designed. Make sure you include a nice headshot on the bio page that you did not have your sister take with the digital camera. Again, keep everything about your book and business strictly professional. And a four-page website should not cost $5,000. If you get quoted that amount run far, far away. Also, when people go to research you for speaking engagements, talk shows and interviews they will reference your website, which builds your expertise and credibility.

Blog – You absolutely should start a blog that supports your overall theme of your book. The blog will keep your website updated and current — and keep the search engine creepy crawlers coming back. What does this do? Move your website up the search engines. What does that do? Keep your name and book out there and at the top of the search engines where prospective buyers can find you. Your blog content should stay on message and be professionally written. Since authors are writers they typically can do this on their own. Our M Communications and 3L blogs review subjects related to … you guessed it … marketing, public relations and books. We also discuss business-related topics. Our blog absolutely works. It pulled both of our websites up to page one on Google, which is exactly what we set out to do. You can also add video and audio blogs. We have our radio show M-Dash radio on our blog and do an audio version of our newsletters and blog. You will also draw in a following

— and perhaps be pleasantly surprised when you have followers from all over the world.

Newsletter – You absolutely should have some sort of tool to drive traffic to your website and blog. You will also want a way to directly reach your subscribers and actively send news and updates for special events such as launch parties or book signings. The newsletter should be electronic — as that is the way most people receive their news. It should NOT be a sales tool. You should be "in service" of your readers and provide useful information related to your book's topic. If your book happens to be a fiction book on crime and punishment — and you're a police detective, then you should focus it on that industry. The idea is to show your expertise to the folks in criminal justice who would hire you to come speak. Just having a newsletter alone can attract speaking engagements. And most importantly you send it out consistently so people become accustomed to receiving it — whether it's once a week, bi-weekly or monthly; but do put it on a schedule and a date of release (e.g., every Monday). You will actually have "fans" if you do it right. They will do things like quote your own newsletter back to you.

Writer's Group ... A.K.A., Big Brains

You will also have to network, and writers' group offer the first place to get comfortable. First, an effective writer's group can help before your book gets published by providing valuable feedback — and not the kind that comes from your Mother or former English teacher. You may have to do some research and sit through some bad meetings to find the one that is right for you; but the writer's community can offer not just support but guidance and inspiration to learn from those who may have gone before you. A terrible writer's group will do the opposite. Here is what to look for when researching a writer's group that is right for you. We recommend you attend a meeting to help you make a decision.

Are leaders published authors? Your writer's group should be led by someone who knows what he or she is doing. A bad sign is that your leader knows less than you do. Someone who has gone before you can provide expertise, guidance and knowledge to help avoid pitfalls and find success. So find out the leader's resume and what it looks like. If she is a pastry chef with no publishing experience who yearns to write her first novel, you might want to keep searching.

Productive critics ... good ... manuscript bashing ... bad. Are the participants a group of angry, frustrated want-to-be writers who have not been published? Do they offer effective and productive critiques of each other's work? Or do you notice that some members take perhaps too much delight in telling Sue her romance novel is sap. Are the participants positive, upbeat, supportive or hopeful? Or are they harsh, direct, snarky or rude? Do they walk in the room and attack someone with, "Why wasn't that listed in your table of contents! A good writer would blah, blah, blah."

Oh that something or another book ... you know ... whatever ... I guess it's selling well (a.k.a., jealousy). You will unfortunately find a few bad apples in the crate when it comes to jealous behavior from your sister writers. For some unknown reason, insecurity runs rampant in this community, and some writers (not all) don't feel anything but resentment and jealousy when you're a success. Maybe it's because they've never been published or their mother dropped them on their heads and told them *they* were clumsy. Who knows — and frankly the only reason you should care is to stay away from groups that have negative behaviors going on. You want a warm, supportive and positive group to help you get where you want to go and support you once you get there.

Political correctness counts only at writer's groups. The next big group behavior that the non-political will not enjoy are writers' groups whose members digress into politics and mudslinging. We've been to writers' groups before where the conversation inevitably turns to politics — and no one writes political books. If you happen to be the lone Republican in the room full of Democrats, watch out. You can even side with their candidate and still be ruefully attacked. So our best suggestion is to keep politics out of discussions about writing. Members that can't abide by that rule ... well give them a flyer for the next Young Democrats meeting and strongly urge them to join that group.

Speakers that provoke thought but don't incite a riot. What kind of speakers come to the group? Are they experienced, knowledgeable experts who give enlightened presentations or do they ramble, lose their way, and end up talking about their favorite red apple at Apple Hill? Or about something called "the core" that to this day we still aren't sure what "the core" means — is it outer or inner as in the apple core in your favorite apple? We don't know. Bad speakers bore, confuse and make you want to run far and away! Good speakers leave you feeling informed and maybe even inspired. Since your time is valuable, don't waste it at groups that invite bad speakers.

Everybody wants to be Famous

The other piece to the marketing puzzle involves networking, book signings and speaking engagements. This trilogy ties together and here is how. You network to get speaking engagements, and speaking engagements come from networking and round and round — and how do book signings fit? Book signings give you a chance to network — and what? Get speaking engagements. Also, be aware that your newsletter and blog will get you speaking gigs too — oh, and, of course your book.

Here is the cool thing about speaking: A great inspirational speech sells LOTS of books. Some writers insist on speaking fees (and times exist when it's appropriate to insist); but passing on a speaking gig because it doesn't pay enough? OK, Holly Golightly … you can't afford to jump in the cab and go to Tiffany's now! You just passed up a huge opportunity to make money from … back of the room sales. We encourage all authors to weigh the return on investment with each speaking gig. It does help your overall endeavor to realize that speaking fees bring income — and that should be factored into your overall success with your book, but never, ever cut off your nose job to spite your facelift. Opportunities from speaking go so much further than back of the room sales too. Other decision makers also see you speak, and word of mouth about your performance spreads. Soon you have numerous speaking offers.

One of our authors very smartly said, "Hey, I'll come speak to your group for free if you'll buy each person a book — and you'll promote me to other organizations." The group gladly accepted the offer in lieu of payment. The author made about $800 on book sales and end up getting asked to speak at the local chamber for $2,000. So, was it worth it to forgo the speaker's fee? Absolutely — he got another gig and it was paid — and he will likely get picked up from that gig to speak elsewhere too. So, don't be shortsighted when it comes to speaker's fees.

Now our all-time favorite comes from an author we'll call Bob Divo. Good old "Bob" had recently complained that the paid speaking gigs were getting fewer and far in between with the economy being what it is. When we went to organize our Writer's Caribbean Cruise, the first author we considered was good old Bob — and did we tell you Bob was a really great speaker too? We approached Bob and offered to pay for his writer's cruise to the Caribbean. Bob, what-are-you-thinking writer with head up you-know-what, agrees with the following conditions: *We must pay for his entire trip including airfare, provide a generous speaker's fee, and (the best part) pay for his entire family of four to join him.* You know what our response to Bob was? Thank you but no thank you.

We probably could understand this better if Bob was a best-selling author whose resume clearly could impress the John Grishams of the world; but Bob is a mid-level author, who does have some nice books out there. He's a good speaker but he's certainly not Superman — now that would be interesting. Superman could give an inspirational talk on why comic-book heroes who risk their lives every day don't get to have disability insurance — those darned unions. And finally, we might even have felt a tad bit sympathetic had Bob not just weeks before been complaining about the lack of speaking gigs. So what's the moral to the story? Don't shit where you cruise … or don't be ridiculous and insist we pay for your family's vacation … *Bob.*

So "Divo" behavior will get you nowhere — and certainly not put you on white-sand beaches in the middle of a cold November. Wonder what Bob will be doing while we party it up on the Lido Deck? Bottom line to all you would-be Bob imitators, don't turn your nose up to any kind of speaking opportunities. Speaking gigs lead to books sales and more speaking opportunities — and more book sales and so on. It really makes zero sense to say "no" over the price of admission. Not to mention that many groups these days are free. Pocketbooks are tight. If you overcharge an event to pay a ridiculous speaker's fee no one shows up. And what we always say is zero of zero equals what? Yeah, simple math that even we can do.

You should also be aware that you have some great multiplication going on here too. One person sees you speak and reads your book — and they're off to tell their friends. Those friends go out and buy the book — again, indirect sales. It's all about momentum and buzz. Authors who put themselves in the spotlight and shine bright can end up being the greatest marketing tool available to help sell their books. Don't be afraid to ask either. If you regularly network with a particular group, ask the leader if you can speak. You can also create a speaker's proposal and when you see opportunities or Request for Speakers and you qualify, do submit your proposal.

Your speaker's proposal should be short and sweet: Introduce yourself, describe your topic, and bullet your takeaways. Here is a basic example of a speaker's proposal:

Dear X,
My name is Michelle Gamble-Risley. I own 3L Publishing, and I'm an author and speaker. My new book Vanity Circus is written to help authors understand the ins and outs of publishing.
I would like to speak to your group of writers on a presentation called Innovations in Publishing. My talk discusses the three main publishing business models: self-publishing, New Publishing and traditional publishing. I will describe how these business models work and outline the pros and cons to each.
Writers will take away:
• an understanding of each publishing model
• a matrix that describes each model's features
• a detailed analysis of which model might work for them
Please let me know if you would like me to come speak to your group.

Best,
Michelle

You may want to ask your marketing person to write one for you — or you may want to allocate some of your PR hours to promoting your speaking skills to large events. Keynote speakers definitely make money. Also, a side note. When you're a keynote speaker, you receive phenomenal exposure. Events usually promote the keynote speaker who has her picture and bio splashed everywhere. The author's book, of course, the highlight and reason she is invited in the first place also gets first-class marketing treatment in the promo. We're talking exposure to perhaps 5,000 to 10,000 attendees and prospective buyers. So, you can see where it pays to speak when it comes to generating endless books sales. And if you're being a Diva about it … we probably won't work with you!

Chapter 13: The Road to Best-Selling Author is paved with Great Publicity

"There is no such thing as bad publicity except your own obituary."
~ Brendan F. Behan

What do you think about the following campaign? Author writes own press release and attempts to secure television coverage, and no one but this tiny little TV station in Podunk, Iowa would pick up the release creatively titled: "New Book Out." New author actually gets on a cable station run by amateur broadcast journalism majors from the local junior college and proceeds to stammer, sweat, fidget and stare at the floor, forgets website address, and book title. In the absence of any significant coverage, the author shows the suspect segment to her parents who despite only catching sight of their daughter's top of head, pat her on the back, and say, "Great spot honey," and then turn and roll their eyes at each other, realizing they are going to have to support their daughter for the rest of her life.

This story comes courtesy to you from our many encounters with what we'll call "Amateur PR 101." Please do yourself and the viewers a favor and hire a publicist. If there is one thing we have heard over and over again at 3L Publishing is the common comment, "I don't need a publicist." Another favorite statement is, "I can do my own public relations." So let us ask you this very simple question: Are you a professional publicist? If the answer here is "no" we are 100 percent sure you will experience one of the following outcomes:

You will not get any coverage.

Your book will sit and gather dust on the shelf.

What does this mean? Zero revenue for you! The bottom line is you are going to need a publicist to make the general public and media aware your book even exists and increase visibility with book consumers. Only cheap fools fall in love with the idea to create a do-it-yourself publicity campaign. Writers partially make this mistake because they figure they can write, so why can't they write their own press release and pitch it? Sounds easy enough, right? Do you know anything at all about media relations? Do you know anything specifically about book pitching? Did you even realize that a pitch about a new book will not likely get airtime or column inches? Do you know what a column inch is? You see our point, right? So let us help you determine how to hire the publicist that will take your unknown book and make it famous.

Because We Said So

Smart Girls:

The caterpillar does all the work but the butterfly gets all the publicity."
~ George Carlin

Basically, you are going to treat this like you are interviewing someone for a job. First, you make sure this person or firm has experience with promoting books. It is a big red flag if someone has healthcare but no book experience. Most publicists specialize in a certain area so beware of the firm that says they can promote *anything and everything* — it simply is not true. We can guarantee you that this person will not have personal relationships with everybody under the sun — and personal relationships are a key to getting media coverage.

You are going to want your publicist to have every book producer and editor contact at all major national media and in the regional markets. With public relations you also can never be guaranteed coverage; however, do ask for references and find out what their track record is. Last, be sure to ask about reporting. Many firms send out a weekly status report that shows coverage and some send out these types of reports monthly.

You are going to want to ask how hours are allocated to what activity, and how they bill as well. Normally, most major firms bill between $3,000 to

$5,000 per month, and the smaller boutiques give you the option to go hourly. Talk to your publicist about your budget, and where and how your hours will be allocated. And, don't forget to ask what happens if you do not get any coverage from a release — a good publicist will stop what they are doing and contact you to immediately switch up the message.

When to Kill the Messenger

Now that we've mentioned "messaging," let's discuss the subject. Your message or press release angle should not be the aforementioned, "Hey gals! We have a new book." Let us be blunt: "Whoopee." Do you have any remote idea how many new books get released daily? Think quadruple digits here. Our joke, "lift a rock, find a writer." Seriously! We're talking thousands. Do you want to know what an editor or producer at *Oprah* or *The Today Show* does when he or she sees a released titled, "New Book Out?" Well, let's just say they don't call. And where does your expensive book (that you probably dumbly sent out without a request for it) and release end up? Hmm, do you suppose the infamous special file? And nothing feels sadder than realizing your book got donated to the Used Book Store in Brooklyn, NY, or worse yet to the local senior center.

A new book announcement should not be about the book per se. It should be the story behind the book or the issue brought up in the book. For example, when 2L's book *Second Bloom* was released in January 2009, the release didn't focus on the book. It was about the New Year and chances to change your life — that release timed with the New Year and issues generated from the recession caused major media outlets to pick up the release and invite 2L to appear on many talk shows. The release clearly was not about the book itself. Another great example comes from authors of the excellent cookbook *Fertile Kitchen*, which got coverage on major NBC affiliates. The story was not about food, but infertility and how good nutrition can enhance your fertility — infertility is a major issue for millions of couples. *Fertile Kitchen* and *Second Bloom* both have themes of hope and happiness. The press releases play up those positive themes without endlessly plugging the book.

If your publicist writes a release announcing your book release, you will know immediately you are in the wrong hands. In fact, you might consider testing your publicist by simply asking, "What would you write if you win this job? If the answer is a pat response, "Well, I would announce the release ..." You are in big trouble. Run fast to another agency.

Good Client Bad Client

> **Smart Girls:**
> "Baby, work it ... Own it!"
> ~ Pretty Woman

Now, let's talk about good client behavior. You are going to want to work with your publicist. Make sure he or she knows what your schedule is. Most of the time when publicists get a bite from the media, he or she needs to make a snap decision, like the client is available or not right then and there to secure the spot. If you are not going to share your schedule and take two days to return your publicist's phone call, we can guarantee you will lose media spots. We once had a client lose three different televisions spots because she took a minimum of two days to respond to media inquiries. Talk about a big fat waste of money. Anyway, please don't show us your low IQ Score and share your schedule.

There are also other ways you can be supporting your publicist's work. Think about what you can be doing virally to support your campaign. Take an active role and participate in social media — whether that is Facebook, LinkedIn or Twitter. The main goal here is to pick which media and be consistent. If you created a fan page or group on LinkedIn, stay consistent and active. Post relevant articles on LinkedIn and always link back to your site. There are also many virtual book clubs you can join as well.

> **Smart Girls:**
> "In Hollywood, an equitable divorce settlement means each party getting 50 percent of publicity!"
> ~ Lauren Bacall

When you hire a publicist, you also are going to want to communicate what your goals are and what area you would like your publicist to focus on. The main ones are: media relations, viral promotion, launch events, book signings and speaking engagements.

We briefly chatted about media relations above (i.e., your publicist knowing everyone having to do with producing book segments), and most authors want this to be the focus of their media campaign. This is how the process works. Your publicist will write a professional press release in the correct format that is accepted by the media. If you do not know what this looks like, and if you notice your release is littered with spelling and grammar errors, you are going to have problems. You approve the written release, and your publicist will send it out to his or her media buddies. You should get a phone call or email if the media has additional questions — and your publicist should have your schedule and be able to book the spot accordingly.

Oh Auntie Em! I Want to Live Forever!

Now, some authors want to be famous and others would rather crawl in a hole or find a nice, safe bunker somewhere than go on television; but nothing destroys a media campaign faster than an unwilling participate. If you don't like the idea of fame then we beg of you: find another profession or just print up 25 copies of your book to give to friends and family. It pains us on a scale of 10 right along with giving birth when a smart girl goes shy girl and avoids the work necessary to make her book succeed — after all your success is our success.

Smart Girls:

"I could be on death row and not have *that* situation."
~ Samantha Jones, Sex in the City the Movie

All you girls deathly afraid of fame or getting a full Brazilian Wax, we recommend you start small and ease into the situation. Your publicist will most likely start with local media so you will be able to practice with the small guys. However, if you are in New York you are not going to have training-wheel time. If you are deathly afraid of television or don't know what to say (like never forgetting to promote your book website or a future appearance) hire a media coach. You will be a pro in no time.

Your publicist can also do viral PR for you. This can be marketing your book on social media if you chose to not do this for yourself, keep your blog current or basically try to get your book listed and reviewed on as many websites as humanly possible. Typically there will be some overlap here, for example, if your publicist markets your book to MORE magazine, they most likely will be promoting to More.com at the same time. Viral PR can also include participation in chat rooms, signing you up for live webcasts, and much more. Basically, your media relations hours are yours to use at your disposal, so the main thing to keep in mind is to communicate consistently with your publicist and he/she will direct you to what is working (getting pick up) and what is not.

> *Smart Girls:*
>
> "Tell me about the rabbits, George."
> ~ Lenny in Of Mice and Men

Now, if you are not an event planner, you are going to want your publicist to plan a launch party for you. Launch parties are a great way to kick start your book sales so if you do not want to have one, let's do a quick reference to that low IQ Rating we just mentioned. Avoiding a book launch party could be compared to taking crisp dollar bills, wiping your mouth on them — dainty dabs if you please — and tossing them in the nearest trash can. You can suddenly see the wasted potential when we put it that way.

When you have a launch party that your publicist plans in full, and if he or she also solicits sponsors, you not only just need to show up you do not have to pay for your event either. Sponsors can be in the form of monetary donations to catering donations for inclusion on your website, in the release, etc. Obviously, your publicist will be sending details of your party to all regional media in a written release.

Your publicist can also schedule signings for you. This is where it becomes really important that you sign with a publisher that has national distribution, because it is really easy to set up signings versus contacting stores on an individual basis. If your book is not distributed it is very difficult to set up signings — and most stores will only schedule on a case-by-case basis.

Last, if you love public speaking and you should … it sells books … ask your publicist to pitch you to the major conferences. This is a great way for you to promote your book, sell your book, and create an additional revenue stream. You will need to send your publicist a bio, any experience, and a video — the major conferences will want to see all of this.

The main point you should take away from this chapter is that you need to hire a publicist or no one will know about your book.

Chapter 14: Hey! That's My Copyright! Isn't it …?"

Nothing will annoy or frustrate a writer more than seeing her work has been republished somewhere else seemingly without her permission. She will go ranting, raving and screaming to all of her friends how she has been ripped off. The publisher is making money off her hard work. She's been victimized — and maybe that is partially true. Yet the truth maybe closer to "She-Writer" didn't review her contract close enough. If you write for a magazine or sold your book to a publisher and didn't read the fine print you may not realize that you respectively sold your North American Serial Rights or your complete copyright to that company. You can complain until you can complain no more because your argument won't stand up in court. The publisher will go right on doing what it's going to do with your manuscript — it legally purchased the copyright.

When you sign a contract with any publisher, please have the agreement reviewed by a lawyer who can fully explains what you are or are not selling. Not all publisher agreements are created equal — and pitfalls exist that may come to bite you in the butt of your super cute designer jeans. You must always take full responsibility for what you put your Jane Hancock on, which means you read it very, very carefully — and if it's a big enough deal where potentially millions of dollars stand to be lost or gained you always have a copyright attorney review your contract. This situation plays an especially important role where licensure of images, games, video games, toys and accessories might come into play. If you sign away all rights to the images, characters and all "accoutrements" and it goes nuclear on the scale of Harry Potter, imagine you're J.K. Rowling who signed away all rights. While her publisher gets rich and acquires true wealth, J.K. sits in her pittance of a million-dollar mansion versus the billion dollar one she could have bought up the street had she not sold away her licensure rights to the characters, film, etc.

Why does this happen in the first place you might be wondering. Sometimes authors get so caught up in the thrill of finding a publisher and being recognized as talent that they just sign wherever and however. No questions asked. The truth is you absolutely must watch your back. Get over the thrill and remember you're not just an artist — you're a business person with business interests to protect. Once you've sold your copyright and anything else away with it, you lose all power. You lose all control. And you live with the results — good, bad or indifferent. If the publisher wants to change you protagonist's name from John to Da-bomb … you're stuck with it. If the publisher wants to change your story from the little girl who fell down the rabbit hole to the space cowboy who gets stuck in the black hole … you're stuck with it. We could give you a dozen more examples.

Now the trade off in traditional publishing is that you don't pay upfront costs and receive royalties. For some people that sounds fabulous; but other writers get a little more upset when their main character's name is changed and the story line shifts. If you don't want that to happen — and to suggest it won't bother you would be lying, because we know from firsthand experience that it will — then don't sell your copyright and use the self publishing or New Publishing model.

Trade Mark ™ Versus Copyright ©

When should you apply for a copyright versus a trademark or both? Your book should always have a copyright, period. As you just saw who owns that copyright is the question, but you must protect your intellectual property (a.k.a., your book) by copyrighting it. You can copyright your material with the U.S. Copyright Office. You send it in and pay a fee, and it's now copyrighted and registered as your property with the U.S. Copyright Office. You can also do the poor girl's copyright and put a copy of your manuscript into a sealed envelope and send it to yourself. Do not open it. Put it away in a locked cabinet somewhere. The date stamp might end up as critical evidence should any disputes come to pass.

Should any question arise or dispute over ownership of the book take place then you can quickly prove when it was copyright protected in a court of law.

Please don't mistakenly believe that you don't need to copyright your material. You must protect it — copyright infringement happens all of the time. If the writer can prove that the publisher read her work and copied it somewhere else then the writer can sue and it goes two ways. The publisher can also take any writer to court who knowingly infringes on the publisher's purchased rights to their book. We realize it sounds really lame that you might actually be sued over your own book, but it happens.

If you have created a screenplay then register and protect it with the Screen Writer's Guild of America. Registration is simple. You can upload and pay for the registration right online. You pay $20 and several weeks later your registration number arrives in the mail. Now some people dispute the validity of the registration process as being a waste of time. You can still get your work stolen — and the Hollywood community doesn't deal with writers very fairly when they bring forth a dispute in court. Truth is you're probably wasting time. Hollywood has a reputation for being unscrupulous and has long since rallied around its own. Writers who dare to go against the system may win — but ultimately lose. They will now be viewed as a liability, and no other studio will openly accept their scripts for fear of a lawsuit. We know it sounds unfair, but we don't want to lie to you. So, registration is good, but should someone steal your work, you have to ask yourself if the risk is worth the result, which could be no further script sales. Of course, we don't want to discourage anyone either. So, you do what you have to do. We have just given you the buyer-beware information.

Now trademark isn't the same as copyright, but similar. You should trademark your title or name if you intend to make a business out of your book. For example, let's assume you might have workshops, seminars, products, T-shirts and any number of other things that might have your name appear on them. A trademark protects the name from being used by unauthorized parties without your permission or payment for use. So, another writer can't go out and write another book with the exact same name when your book has a trademark — and please note: The placement of the ™ symbol on any title shows the "intent" to trademark. So long before you ever make the trademark official you can place the appropriate symbol and demonstrate your intention, which should ward off rip-off artists.

It's my Copyright I'll Whine if I Want to

You might be able to negotiate special agreements with your publisher regarding copyright. You can put special stipulations in your contract to override problems such as changing the name of the book or having the ability to approve the cover, etc. If you ever saw the episode of *Sex and the City* where Carrie Bradshaw realizes her head is about to be superimposed on a naked woman's body bare on the streets of New York then you know she had the right to refuse. Is Carrie's situation the norm? No, it depends on the agreement. In Carrie's case she must have had the right to approve the cover.

Writers just need to be aware that a contract can be negotiated to their satisfaction; but also realize they walk a fine line. Not all publishing houses will willingly give away that much power on material they may be spending top dollar to purchase and produce. If you happen to be Suzie Q. Nobody you will be especially vulnerable to the publisher's demands to do it a certain way. Why? You have no track record to stand on as a pulpit for why you know more than they do. Publishers don't have a lot of time to argue with writers. If you become particularly defensive and demanding you also risk them pulling the plug. The writing is on the manuscript at that point. If you're a PITA now chances are PITA behavior will not cease and desist after the book lands on the bookstore shelves — and nobody likes to work with a PITA. So just realize that you should be open minded and perhaps respect the publisher's expertise and knowledge of the market.

In All Fair Use

Now before any writer freaks out because their book got quoted somewhere or another writer referenced their work without their permission, please be familiar with what's called "fair use." Fair use is a clause of U.S. Copyright Law that applies four principles to determine infringement. To explain "fair use," we're going to use it to define it by pulling the principles from Wikiquote: "The purpose and character of the use, including whether the use is of a commercial nature or is for nonprofit, educational purposes; the nature of the copyrighted work; the amount and substantiality of the portion used in relation to the copyrighted work as a whole; and the effect of the use upon the potential market for or value of the copyrighted work."

A general rule of thumb to understand fair use in a basic sense: If someone pulls a sentence, quote or paragraph from your work without taking the whole of the work they have used it "fairly." Now if you've pulled entire chapters or even a significant number of paragraphs, you may be in violation of copyright. You must always give credit to the original author and not pull the information and then put your name on it. At the very least when you credit the author you will most likely avoid any problems or dispute — as long as you have not pulled the whole and only used a fraction of the work. Also, if you're truly concerned, always run it by an attorney. You do not want to end up in court over some silly dispute when it could have been easily avoided.

First Right of Refusal

Some poor schmucks get taken for the ultimate rip-off by signing contracts where the publisher employs the infamous *First Right of Refusal.* Now in all fairness to publishers, they have that clause in place just in case you do turn into the next Stephenie Meyer. Who can blame them? They will want to protect what they feel is a franchise they established; however, here comes the super lame part. First Right of Refusal sucks big time when the publisher doesn't produce for the author — and the author is officially stuck in this purgatory publishing hell. The author doesn't want to work with the publisher anymore yet this clause precludes their pursuit of a new publisher that they could forge a new relationship.

What we recommend is the author approaches the publisher to see if the dispute can be resolved amicably. Call your publisher and ask for a meeting. Don't go ballistic, get angry or irrational. Sit down with your publisher and see if you can dissolve the agreement. Most publishers know if the relationship has gone south — and one would hope that the publisher is probably aware the author isn't happy with the results. You should calmly and logically ask to be released from the obligation.

The better advice suggests you don't enter into this kind of arrangement at all. If your publisher has this clause in your contract, request it be removed.

If they refuse to remove it simply ask them why not? If you have no history or track record to show that you have the next Harry Potter just explain that you would like to publish one book with them and determine upon its release and results whether or not this relationship will work for you; but being forced into a relationship with a publisher for the long term doesn't always make sense. So, carefully consider these kinds of clauses before you automatically sign on the dotted line.

Love Letter

We love authors! You may have read *Vanity Circus* and perhaps wondered why we're even in this business; but the truth is we love the whole industry. We launched 3L Publishing out of a genuine interest in changing the process for the better — and changing it more in the author's favor. We kept hearing dozens of horror stories and wondered why it was more lucrative to write a magazine article for $2 a word versus an entire book that could take up to several years to end up being paid mere pennies per hour. It didn't seem fair or appropriate. So as authors we realized things needed to change. We realize that a handful of authors go on to make their fortune with a best seller; but more often than not the vast majority end up writing wonderful books that don't sell not because of the book's quality, but because the author simply doesn't have the business knowledge or marketing and PR savvy to make it sell, so it sits and gathers dust.

We believe that with this knowledge, and the changes we've made to the publishing process that our authors will at the very least be able to make a good if not a great living at what they love doing. We can't promise anyone their book will become a best seller. We can't promise we will make you rich; but we can promise that you will have a beautiful and well-written book that we will do everything within our power to make a success — and sometimes success is defined by just the act of getting it published with a fabulous launch party.

We do hope that as 3L grows and we add new authors — and the industry stands up and takes notice — that perhaps in the end we will have done a really great thing for authors. We will have made necessary changes and set up programs where authors really are in a position to truly realize decent royalties and return on investment. We hope that becoming an author will pay off and attract more talented individuals to join the growing rank of writers who don't have the odds so stacked against them it is nearly impossible to make money. We hope you will all find a 3L Publishing that willingly takes a stand against mediocrity; creates fair and equitable publishing practices; doesn't force writers to sign away their copyrights in exchange for nothing; doesn't demand an agent represent you and take 10 percent; and doesn't send you off to find a publicist that you must pay some expensive retainer just to get mentioned in the local community news. We believe in our authors, but more importantly we believe in the power of words and messages to change the world. And we believe that 3L Publishing is blazing a New Publishing standard where everybody wins!

Smart Girls:

"Who doesn't enjoy oogling bad book covers."
~ Samantha, Sex in the City

About the Authors

Michelle Gamble-Risley (left) is an award-winning author, speaker and business owner of M Communications (www.mcommunicationsinc.com) and 3L Publishing (www.3LPublishing.com). *Vanity Circus* is her third book and the third in the Smart Girl's Guide series. She has been working as a professional writer, editor and marketing specialist for 20 years. She wrote *Vanity Circus* to help authors everywhere avoid doing what the cover aptly suggests — publishing crap. She hopes authors will take the book's words of advice and avoid the pitfalls and heartaches often associated with publishing.

Michele Smith (right) is an award-winning marketing professional, author, speaker and business owner of M Communications and 3L Publishing. *Vanity Circus* is her second book she published with her business partner, Michelle-Gamble Risley. She wrote *Vanity Circus* to educate authors about the publishing industry and to provide valuable insight for authors trying to navigate the waters. As a seasoned publicist, her clients have appeared on many national television and radio broadcast programs. Michele has been featured on the *Rachael Ray Show, ABC National News* as well as in national magazines.

Books from 3L Publishing

To order, visit www.3Lpublishing.com

3L Publishing provides complete publishing services to help authors, individuals and businesses take their manuscripts or custom publications and turn them into beautiful, perfect-bound books. We offer premier writing, editorial, production and marketing and public relations services for authors looking for a publisher to produce their books; individuals wanting an idea transformed into a publishable book; and businesses seeking experienced writers and editors to produce manuals, guides and custom publications, reports and papers.

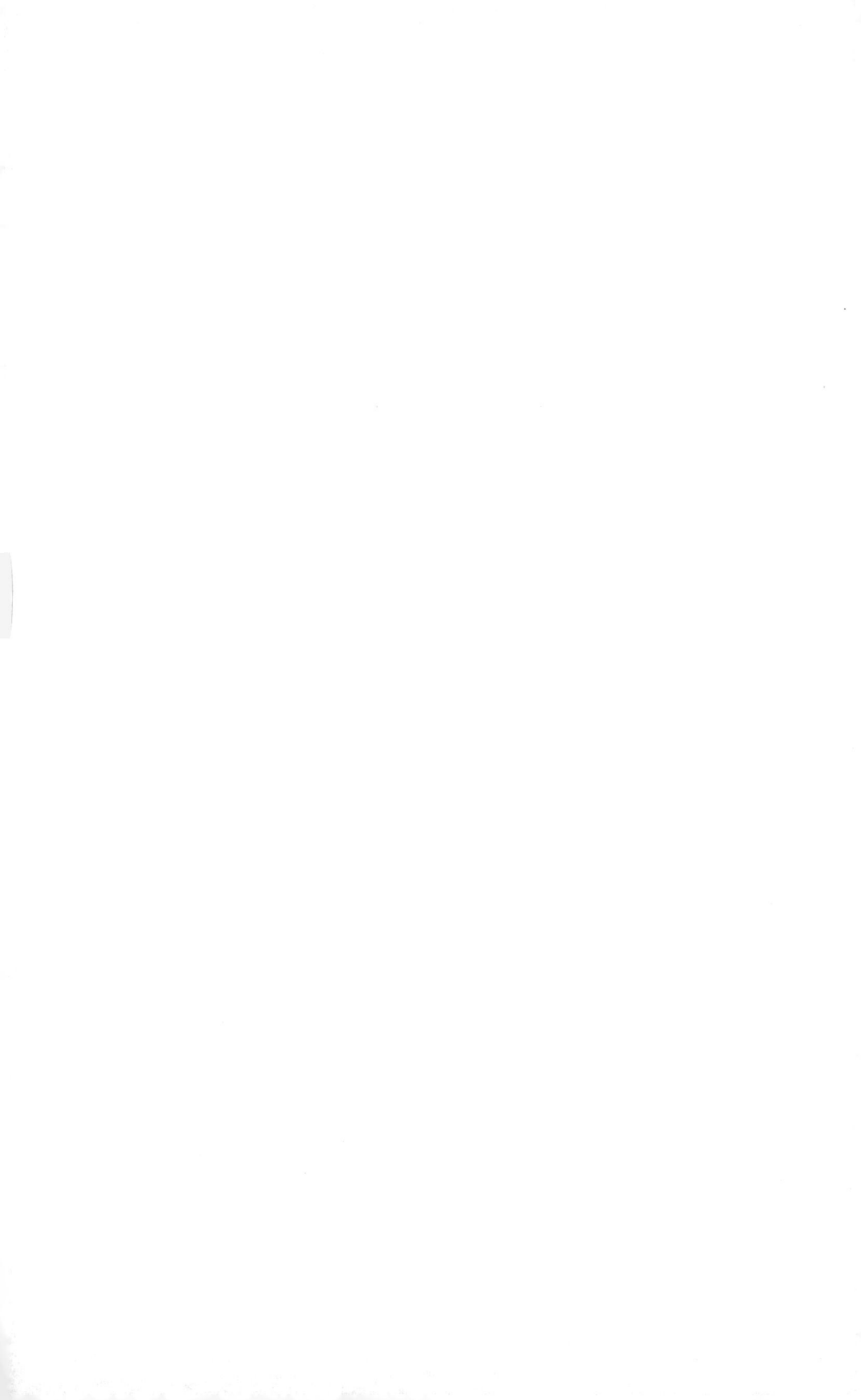